To Peter & Melia
with love & best wishes from
Adrian

THE GOLDEN CALVES
OF JEROBOAM

& OTHER REFLECTIONS

ADRIAN LEAK

Adrian Leak 29. 9. 20

The Book Guild Ltd

First published in Great Britain in 2020 by
The Book Guild Ltd
9 Priory Business Park
Wistow Road, Kibworth
Leicestershire, LE8 0RX
Freephone: 0800 999 2982
www.bookguild.co.uk
Email: info@bookguild.co.uk
Twitter: @bookguild

Typeset in Aldine401 BT

Printed and bound in Great Britain by CPI Group (UK) Ltd, Croydon, CR0 4YY

ISBN 978 1913208 837
British Library Cataloguing in Publication Data.
A catalogue record for this book is available from the British Library.

To my Grandchildren
William, James, Henry, Eleanor and Tiberius
With love

CONTENTS

SKETCHES

ENVOIE

PREFACE

Dear Reader,

William Gladstone, the Victorian statesman, remembered overhearing on a stagecoach journey a conversation between two fellow passengers. 'Well, what *is* the Church of England, then?' said one. 'The Church of England,' said the other, 'is a damn big building with an organ inside.' Gladstone dined out on that story for the rest of his life.

Defining the Church is best done tentatively, if at all. Even then, what is the point? To define is to set limits, and we should be wary of boundaries. The lives of the people around us give us a boundless horizon, and it is there that we find unexpected glimpses of glory.

'As kingfishers catch fire' so Christ's grace flashes through our world, skimming across our provisional boundaries of creed and race. Now and then, here and there, it dazzles us in the words and actions of friends and strangers, not only of those alive today, but also of those who now rejoice 'upon another shore and in a greater light'.

In this collection of articles and sermons I hope that you will find something to gladden your heart; some words, perhaps, to lighten your spirits as you settle for sleep at the close of a busy day. Do not look for any theme or grand design: there is none, except the rich, confused and multi-layered experience of our daily lives.

For that reason you will find jumbled together within the narrow compass of this slim volume not only scented candles and broiled fish but also the man who paved the quagmire of Piccadilly; the great Maimonides, rabbi of ancient Cairo;

the haberdasher of East Grinstead; the Victorian lady who pioneered social housing; 'Alison', who was excoriated by Graham Norton for her ingratitude; the indomitable Miss Sheen who taught us to dance the military two-step; the Venetian consul's wife who played the mandolin; and many others too.

Dip in from time to time.

Adrian Leak
Guildford
Surrey

THE GOLDEN CALVES OF JEROBOAM

(First published in the *Church Times*, January 2020.)

The Golden Calves of Jeroboam was a phrase which cropped up from time to time in our childhood games of charades. Having given the conventional signal for a quotation and indicated with five fingers the number of words, it required no great acting skill to denote the second word (one of the grown-ups in the room was bound to be wearing a wedding ring) and the third word needed no more than a tap on the back of the leg below the knee. By then someone – possibly the whole room – would have shouted, 'The golden calves of Jeroboam,' which was just as well, because no one had ever worked out how to mime the word 'Jeroboam'.

The choice of a biblical subject might suggest that we were an unusually pious family, but that was not the case. The golden calves belonged to that stock of half-remembered stories and characters from the Bible, which was still common currency in many households during the first half of the twentieth century. When the situation called for it we alluded to the immutable laws of the Medes and the Persians; at times we spoke wistfully of the years that the locusts had eaten; and when we passed on a bit of gossip, we were careful to add the rider, 'Tell it not in Gath'.

In those days biblical quotations cropped up everywhere. Even Hugh 'Bulldog' Drummond, the hero of 'Sapper's' novels, still popular in the 1950s, was moved in a moment of high emotion to quote from scripture. In reply to his friend Toby's remark, 'You'll be getting married, old bean,' Drummond replied, 'True, O King.' (Daniel 3: 24)

In popular culture the Bible shared precedence with Shakespeare. In the radio programme *Desert Island Discs*, the castaway was allowed to have a volume of Shakespeare and a copy of the Bible, a tradition which, oddly, endures to this day. In the first broadcast (1942) the entertainer, Vic Oliver, was invited to be Roy Plomley's castaway. That an Austrian Jew, brought up in the traditions of a Viennese synagogue, should be offered the Christian Bible did not strike anyone as at all odd. It was taken for granted by the BBC that no English-speaking castaway should be deprived of such a resource, for the Bible was not considered the exclusive property of Christianity. It belonged with Shakespeare to the wider constituency of British culture.

Popular English authors of the first half of the twentieth century – writers like John Buchan, P G Wodehouse, Dornford Yates, Dorothy L Sayers and H C McNeile (Sapper) – were able to dip into a reservoir of quotations from the Bible, confident that their allusions would be familiar to their readers.

When Ian Fleming recreated Captain Hugh Drummond in the character of Commander James Bond, he borrowed a number of recognisable features: the hero was a well-tailored and understated old Etonian, a connoisseur of fine wines and fast cars, and useful with his fists. The villain was a nasty foreigner, or if not foreign, a man of uncertain parentage, who cheated at cards and had links with a world of international crime. In many ways Bond was interchangeable with Drummond, and Auric Goldfinger with Carl Peterson. In many ways, but not in all: Bond, for all his superficial gloss, was definitely not a gentleman.

There was another gulf between Drummond's world and Bond's. James Bond was unlikely to quote from the Bible or Shakespeare. The role did not require it and it would have been unconvincing if it had. By 1953, when Fleming published his first Bond novel, the world had changed since Drummond's first appearance in 1920, and those two foundation texts of the English language – three if you include the Book of Common Prayer – although still hidden deep beneath the surface of our culture, were no longer recognised or openly acknowledged.

That was how it was in the 1950s. Now, seventy years later in 2020, anyone wishing to communicate with a popular readership cannot assume their readers to have any knowledge whatsoever of the Bible. This means that for the first time in five centuries the Church of England must learn to speak to a nation for which the Bible is a closed book.

Without the ambience of a biblically literate culture, unchurched couples wanting a church wedding will be puzzled by references in their service to 'Christ's bride' and the wedding at Cana. No less of a worry will be the allusion at their child's christening to the waters of the Red Sea. These biblical associations, once generally understood, are now no longer intelligible to an unchurched population. They need explaining, but allusions that need to be explained miss the point, which is that they should *not* need explanation.

This presents us with a problem. It is the same one which confronted St Paul in Athens. Contrary to his usual practice of preaching within the tradition of the Jewish scriptures and appealing to converts from the synagogue, he tried on that occasion to preach a sermon outside the biblical context. It did not work. There was a complete breakdown in communication. The Gospel was not rejected: it was not 'heard'. The people on the Areopagus that day simply did not get it, and were never likely to do so, as without the context of biblical Judaism it simply made no sense.

In our country we are now in the same position. We believe that 'God so loved the world that he gave his only begotten son, to the end that all that believe in him should not perish, but have everlasting life', but to proclaim this amazing truth to people who have little or no knowledge at all of the biblical concepts of sin and redemption is likely to be as ineffective as St Paul's appeal to the Athenians. An earlier generation born in the 1930s, many of whom were used to collective worship at school and church parade during national service, may have groaned at compulsory religion, but at least their upbringing gave them a familiarity with the language and concepts of a biblical culture. That generation is now rapidly disappearing.

As a parish priest, like most of my colleagues, I relied on the occasional populist service to bring in new families while still trying to keep the attendance of the 'regulars'. The liturgical calendar provided opportunities to have a 'special service' almost every other month at which I could add bells and whistles to the basic narrative of the church's year. This is perhaps the universal practice among parish clergy.

But, as we are always being told, success measured by numbers can be deceptive. Looking back at my own ministry I suspect that I strove too hard to fill the pews with the many who were not there, and not hard enough to teach the few who were. I went for the easier alternative to the hard slog of patient teaching with its undeniably slow results.

Jeroboam seemed to offer that easier alternative. By setting up those golden calves to seduce the Israelites from worshipping the true God, he presented an attractive but superficial 'quick fix'. Aaron had done the same centuries before. It was the same old story: 'Here are your gods, O Israel, who brought you up out of the land of Egypt'. Instead of travelling the hard road and being prepared to lose some disciples on the way, the Israelites looked to Jeroboam who offered the easier path.

SLEEPERS, WAKE!

'Wake up!' said the preacher, as the people shuffled their feet in the straw and prayed that he would be brief. 'It's time you woke up. Now. NOW! WAKE UP!', and he thumped the pulpit with his fist.

The year was 1503, the month December, and because it was the first Sunday of Advent there was a sermon. The preacher came from the priory in the nearby town and was well known in the local villages for his improvised preaching. Most of the parishes in that region were served by Mass priests, unlicensed to preach. A sermon was a rare diversion.

He warmed to his theme. Waiting for the coughing to subside, he then pointed to the painting on the chancel arch. It depicted in lurid colours the Great Assize, a scene of terrifying realism in which Christ sat in judgement, dismissing with his left hand the souls of the wicked into the jaws of hell, and welcoming with his right the souls of the blessed into paradise.

'Look,' the preacher declaimed, and this time he contrived to add a tremor to his voice. 'And look well' – he paused and seemed almost to leap from the pulpit – 'THERE IS YOUR DOOM.'

The more attentive of the congregation shifted uneasily as they remembered St Paul's text from his Epistle to the Romans, which the preacher had recited in English earlier in the Mass, while the celebrant had mumbled it in Latin:

The night is far spent, the day is at hand: let us therefore cast off the works of darkness, and let us put on the armour of light. Let us walk honestly, as in the day; not in rioting and drunkenness, not in chambering and wantonness, not in strife and envying. ★

5

Who could escape the wrath to come? Surely he was laying it on a bit thick. An occasional outbreak of rioting and drunkenness did no one any harm, as long as one paid for the damage, and as for a bit of chambering and wantonness, well, one was only human after all. Were they all to perish in the flames?

The question lingered in their minds. Then the preacher's voice suddenly changed and his face, so dark with foreboding, was now transfigured with a beaming smile. 'Ah, my dear friends,' and he stretched out his arms to embrace them all. 'My dear, dear brothers and sisters, let us look away from the dark. Let us turn to the light. The day is at hand. Look!' – and he pointed across the church to the Lady Chapel with its statue of Mary holding up the infant Christ – 'Look there! THERE IS YOUR SALVATION.'

That same year, 1503, and not many miles away, a fourteen-year-old lad from Nottinghamshire enrolled as an undergraduate at Jesus College, Cambridge. His name was Thomas Cranmer. On Advent Sunday in the college chapel he heard the same Pauline text, with its startling juxtaposition of dark and light, judgement and mercy. Fluent in Latin, like all his fellow students, he did not need an English paraphrase or painted image. He was trained to apprehend the mysteries of faith through words, not pictures.

Many years later, as an old man in his sixties, Cranmer would have known much of the daily Office by heart. He had been reciting it every day since his ordination. The texts and prayers which formed a priest's regular devotion were among the sources he worked upon to create the Book of Common Prayer in 1549. For Advent Sunday he set as the Epistle the same passage from St Paul's Letter to the Romans as he had heard forty six years earlier in the Jesus College chapel. For the Collect he composed an elegantly balanced prayer which combined the two Advent themes of the First and Second Coming of Christ:

Almighty God give us grace that we may cast away the works of darkness, and put upon us the armour of light, now in the time of this mortal life, in which thy Son Jesus Christ came to visit us in great humility; that in the last day, when he shall come again in his glorious majesty to judge both the quick and the dead, we may rise to the life immortal, through him who liveth and reigneth with thee and the Holy Ghost, now and ever.**

This Collect is one of the jewels of the Anglican liturgy. To the reader, to the listener, but above all to the worshipper, it opens out like a medieval diptych, its twin panels hinged by the words *that in the last day*. It holds before our eyes the two dazzling icons of our salvation: Christ's nativity at Bethlehem when 'he visited us in great humility', and his Second Coming 'when he shall come again in his glorious majesty to judge both the quick and the dead'.

---

*   They would have heard this passage spoken in the Middle English dialect current at that time:

We know this tyme that the owre now is com that we ought to rise fro slepe for now owre helthe is nere. The nyght went before, but the day hath nyghede. Therfore caste we awey the werkis of derkenesse and be clothed with the armor of lyghte. As in a day walke we honestly; not in superflue of festis and dronkennessis, not in beddis and unchastiteis, not in strife and in envy, but be ye clothed in the Lorde Ihesu Criste.

(A Late Fifteenth Century Dominican Sermon Cycle
vol 1, pp 7-9, ed Stephen Morrison EETS 2012.)

**Our modern Anglican liturgy (*Common Worship 2000*) retains Cranmer's Collect for Advent Sunday, adding as a post-communion option an ancient prayer from the Gelasian Sacramentary, one of Cranmer's sources. It also provides in the three-year cycle of recommended readings for the Eucharist the pre-Reformation choice of Romans 13.

Hark, a thrilling voice is sounding;
'Christ is nigh,' it seems to say;
'cast away the dreams of darkness,
O ye children of the day.'

THE SCENTED CANDLE FIASCO

(From a sermon preached at Withyham Parish Church
on Christmas Day 2008.)

In our house the customary merriment of Christmas was almost derailed by the fiasco of the scented candle.

We had decided that we were going to be sensible about presents. A ceiling – and I am bound to say that it was a rather low ceiling – was placed on the cost of each present. It was going to be a minimalist Christmas; spare but stylish. Our giving was to be based on the principle that one single chocolate truffle by Charbonnel et Walker (hand-crafted and beautifully wrapped) is smarter than a whole box of Milk Tray.

Well, that was the theory. But we had not reckoned on the dire impact that one single scented candle (hand-crafted and beautifully wrapped) would make upon our festive joy.

We had been invited by friends to dinner. It was a week or so before Christmas, and we took with us our well-chosen gift. 'How exciting,' our hostess cried, 'but you really shouldn't have, you know.' And as we mumbled words of self-deprecation, she called out to her husband, 'Charles, just look what Josephine and Adrian have brought us.' Behind them we caught a glimpse through the sitting-room door of our fellow guests turning to behold our late arrival and this much-heralded and wondrous gift.

'I'll tell you what,' our hostess continued – there was no stopping her – 'I won't open it now. I'll put it under the tree, and then we can open it on Christmas morning with the family. So *exciting*. I love Christmas surprises, don't you?'

ADRIAN LEAK

Later at dinner, during a lull in the chatter, she asked whether we had read Victoria Mather's latest 'Social Stereotypes' column. 'You must. It's absolutely spot on.' She fetched the paper and began to read. It was, as you would expect, a witty and devastating demolition of the whole scented candle phenomenon. Laugh? My goodness, how we laughed! Meanwhile, our little gift (hand-crafted and beautifully wrapped) sat silently beneath the Christmas tree, a time bomb of embarrassment waiting to go off on Christmas morning.

There is an art in giving and an art in receiving. Giving an inappropriate gift can be an embarrassment. Receiving an unwanted gift can be a challenge. 'How kind; thank you so much,' we say politely, but the giver knows that our heart is not in it.

God's gift to the world at Bethlehem was certainly unexpected, and to a large extent unwanted. Almost, you might say, an embarrassment. Or so it would seem two thousand years after that astonishing event. A new-born baby with his young mother in a poor and lowly stable, the oxen standing by. The story, so familiar, never fails to tug at our heartstrings. And yet, and yet… Do we miss the point?

What, then, should be our response? Wonder, of course. Reverence, yes, that too, and hope; hope for a better world, a world of peace and goodwill for all. But there is something else. Something more than wistful longing. Something hard to hear over the sounds of Christmas celebration.

It's what Mary heard when, a few weeks later, she took her baby to be blessed in the Temple, and that good old man Simeon warned her that a sword of grief would pierce her heart. It's what the Wise Men meant when as well as gold and frankincense they included among their gifts myrrh, a symbol of sorrow and mourning.

There will be a time for us, too, to hear that slower tune (but not now); a time to turn our faces with Jesus towards his Calvary (but not yet). Not now, not yet, because it is his dancing day. And he has called us to the dance in the words of the old carol:

Tomorrow shall be my dancing day;
I would my true love did so chance,
To see the legend of my play,
To call my true love to my dance.
Sing, oh! my love, oh! my love, my love, my love,
This have I done for my true love.

BROILED FISH AND HONEYCOMB

(From a sermon preached at Withyham Parish Church
on the Third Sunday of Easter 2006.)

*They gave him a piece of a broiled fish, and of an honeycomb.
And he took it, and did eat before them.*

(Luke 24: 42, 43)

Is there not something wonderful about fish? I do not mean
the exotic multi-coloured ones which swim round and round
in their ornamental bowls. I mean the fish that lies upon your
dinner plate; the fish that you delicately dissect, skin from
flesh, flesh from bone, before you pop each delicious morsel
into your mouth. This is the fish which not only delights your
palate and satisfies your hunger but, we are assured, brings
health to body, mind and soul.

There is something miraculous about the chain of events
which links you to your supper, your supper to the fish market,
the fish market to the dock, and thence to the trawler and the
shoals of cod, herring, halibut and bream swimming in the
ocean.

The fish which the risen Christ ate that evening with his
disciples – the one he ate before their eyes to demonstrate that
it was indeed he who stood before them and not an apparition
– that fish had almost certainly been caught some days earlier
in the Sea of Galilee.

At the time of that event the disciples were in Jerusalem,
and so it was unlikely that they would be eating fresh fish.
Without refrigeration, any fish eaten in Jerusalem which had

been transported across country to the market from Galilee would have been salted or pickled. In fact, in the Roman world of that time the small Galilee fish, no bigger than a sardine, was a popular dish throughout the empire, but particularly in Palestine.

In the story of the Feeding of the Five Thousand, when the boy was asked to share his packed lunch of five barley loaves and two small fish, the fish would have been the little pickled ones from Galilee. There were other times when Jesus and his disciples would have eaten their fish fresh from the sea, as when after his resurrection he stood on the shore, watching the disciples at work in their fishing boats. 'Come and have breakfast,' he called out to them. When they came ashore he was already grilling some fish on a beach fire. How good that must have smelt and tasted to those tired men who had been working all night in their boats.

For those men whose trade was to harvest and sell fish, there was a strong bond between themselves and the natural order of Creation. Their livelihood and their food was there, swimming in the water alongside and beneath the hulls of their boats. And the farmer who sowed his crops, and the vine-dresser who pruned his vines, and the shepherd who went looking for his lost sheep, and the carpenter's son at Nazareth who knew the feel and smell of different woods and their distinct properties (broad grain pine for furniture, close grain olive for cups): for all of them there was a close affinity with their environment and the material of existence, the colour, touch and smell of the living world; sheep, goats, fish, figs, grapes, wheat, rivers, rocks, seas, mountains, trees, people.

In the Bible, humanity is continuous with the environment she inhabits. People are not depicted as observers of nature, nor as plunderers or conservers. They are not bystanders, distinct from creation. They are part of it.

Nowhere is our continuity with our habitat more clearly shown than by our need to eat. We eat our environment and, in due time, when our bodies fail and are of no more use, they in turn are eaten by the world which once sustained them. We are taken back into the ground from which we came. We are wrong to shudder, as we might, at the sentence which will be spoken over our dead bodies: 'earth to earth, ashes to ashes, dust to dust', for these are not words of dark despair, but of hope. In the long perspective of faith they are ablaze with the fire of the Creator's love.

When God willed the redemption of his world, he became one with it and lived a human life. His incarnation, which began in the womb of Mary, did not cease to unfold at his birth. The miracle was not confined to a single episode. It was continuous. The process of incarnation (enfleshment) went on every day throughout Christ's earthly life. What makes you and me the unique individuals we are is not a single event which happened unseen in our mother's womb. It is so much more than that. It is transition, not event; a continuous development contemporary with our daily living as we progress from womb to tomb.

So it was with Jesus Christ. God became incarnate not only by the message of an angel, but through his upbringing by his parents, the conversation of the grown-ups he overheard, the instruction of the rabbis, the affection of his friends, the skills he learnt in the workshop, the people he encountered in Galilee, the air he breathed, the ground he trod and always, every day, the food he ate.

During his incarnate life in Palestine, God was drawn by his food into the fabric of the material world. By his resurrection and ascension, the fabric of this world has been and is being drawn back into the very life of God – and that includes the broiled fish he ate and the piece of honeycomb he relished.

ST JOSEPH OF NAZARETH

(From a sermon preached at St Alban's Church, Wood Street Village, Guildford, on the First Sunday of Christmas 2001.)

There is one person in the Bethlehem story who never seems to get into the limelight and who is forever in the background, upstaged by Mary, the baby Jesus, shepherds, wise men and angels. And yet, for all that, he is a key figure in the Christmas story.

I mean, of course, Joseph: Joseph, the carpenter; Joseph, Mary's husband; Joseph, Jesus's earthly father. We know very little about him. We are told that he was betrothed to Mary. Betrothal in those days meant more than our modern engagement to marry. A betrothed couple were closer to marriage than an engaged couple. Betrothal was part of the process of marriage itself.

We can imagine, therefore, the shock Joseph must have felt, the dreadful dismay, when Mary told him that she was expecting a baby. What could he do? He knew that he was not the father. The Jewish law was clear and cruel. A woman found guilty of breaking her vows of betrothal by becoming pregnant by another man was sentenced to death by stoning.

Joseph decided to keep quiet and divorce Mary before her condition became public knowledge. But then he had a dream in which God told him that Mary had been chosen to bear the Son of God; that this forthcoming birth was not a catastrophe and a disgrace, but a miraculous intervention.

God gave Joseph the task of giving the child his name. Name-giving in the biblical tradition was a sacred duty. Again and again in the Bible a person is given a name to describe his or her status or vocation. Naming someone was in some cases done by God's direct command. For example, God changed Abram's name to Abraham, and Jacob's to Israel. More often it was the father who conferred the name on his infant son. Joseph's kinsman, Zechariah, was commanded by God to name his son John – the one who grew up to become John the Baptist.

Joseph was commanded by God to call his son 'Jesus', which meant 'Saviour'. In naming the baby who was to become the Christ, Joseph was being drawn into God's design for the world's salvation.

Then Joseph had another dream and further instructions. 'Take the child and his mother,' said God, 'and flee to Egypt, and remain there until I tell you; for Herod is about to search for the child to destroy him.'

In these two dreams, in which God gives instructions about the naming of Jesus and about his escape from the murderous Herod, Joseph is centre stage. But thereafter he moves into the background and Mary takes on the predominant role. When the parents take their infant son to present him at the Temple, it is Mary who is addressed by Simeon, who declares that her child will grow up to be a leader of Israel. And later, when they take Jesus to Jerusalem and he gives them the slip so that he can listen to the teaching of the rabbis in the Temple, it is Mary, not Joseph, who rebukes the boy: 'Child, why have you treated us like this? Look, your father and I have been searching for you everywhere.'

There is one further reference to Joseph after this. On an occasion when Jesus has returned to his hometown and preached in the local synagogue, the people are astonished. 'Isn't this Joseph's son – isn't this the carpenter's boy?' they say, amazed and rather affronted.

After that, we hear no more of Joseph. We are not told what happened to him, whether he grew old in Nazareth or died before his son. We do not know if he became a disciple, as Mary did. Because Mary appears to be living alone, so that on the cross Jesus commends her to John's protection, the tradition is that Joseph was much older than her and predeceased her by many years.

What we do know is this: Joseph was chosen by God to carry out the role of fatherhood, to honour and protect his young wife, to bring up his son, to be a sure and loving presence in the home at Nazareth, and to do that most difficult thing: to allow the boy to grow up and to become a bigger man than him.

It is our vocation as parents to be outshone by our children. For a while, and not for very long, we are indispensable to them. Then we must step aside.

Joseph knew when to step aside.

CHRISTMAS PRESENTS

(A sermon preached at Withyham Parish Church on Christmas Day 2010.)

Soon you will be opening your presents. Fingers will be stripping off the sticky tape, untying the knots, ripping open acres of wrapping paper. And then come the little shrieks of excitement – 'Goodness, how *lovely* – isn't that just *wonderful* – thank you *so* much' – and you kiss and hug. Everyone is caught up in the exchange of gifts. As the Bible says: 'Young men and maidens, old men and children, and the stranger within your gates.'

Of course, no Christmas is without its disappointments. We learn from experience how to conceal them with a good grace. You hoped he would give you something sparkly and fun: a bracelet, perhaps, or a ring. How hard it is to feign true joy over a pair of oven gloves.

Hear what happened one Christmas to Alison (no, not that Alison; the other one). She found that instead of the bracelet she had hoped for, her nice boyfriend had bought her a fountain pen. This cast a shadow over the festive fun. She began to brood over the matter and decided to write to *The Daily Telegraph* – to be more specific, to Graham Norton's Agony Column.

Now that was a mistake. Someone should have told Alison that Graham Norton has a short, sharp way with self-pitying whingers. This was his reply:

Dear Alison. He got you a pen. You wanted a bracelet. You are 'incredibly disappointed'? You are aware that the country is at war? Have you heard anyone mention the economic

meltdown? Be thrilled that someone has bothered to buy you
anything. One last plea – please don't use your beautiful new
*pen to write to me ever again.**

Poor Alison.

I suppose that there are times when we all need that
rebuke. Times when we are quick to assess the value of the
gift but slow to appreciate the affection of the giver. Knowing
as we do how curmudgeonly and ungracious we often are, it
should come as a pleasant surprise that anyone should take the
trouble to select, buy, wrap and send us a gift at all.

So much for the art of receiving, but what about the art of
giving? Here we come to the issue of recycling unwanted gifts.

Every home has a secret drawer holding a collection
of duplicates and unwanted gifts awaiting recycling to
unsuspecting cousins. *Schott's Miscellany* is there. So is Barbara
Cartland's slim volume on social etiquette. And do you
remember Lynn Truss's *Eats, Shoots and Leaves*? A friend of
ours marked his unwanted second copy before recycling it to
an aunt in Market Harborough and was rather surprised when
he received it back the following year. He was even more
surprised when, next to the minute tell-tale mark he had made
on the inside cover, he found a second, identical one. 'Makes
you lose your faith in human nature,' he grumbled.

The truth is that human nature, even in its happier
aspects, is somewhat blemished. Our generosity is rarely
unconditional. Our spontaneity is often contrived. And so
what we need once a year to remind us of the true nature of
giving is the great festival of Christ's birth. Today we celebrate
God's unconditional gift to the human race. He gives us
himself.

---

* Quoted by kind permission of Graham Norton.

God so loved the world that he gave his only begotten son, to the end that all that believe in him should not perish but have everlasting life.

Belief in Christ, that little baby in the manger, gives us a foretaste of heaven. We join so many others as we kneel in the straw at Bethlehem: the shepherds and the magi on that first occasion, and since then a great crowd of Christmas pilgrims; captains and kings, rich and poor, achievers and losers, Alison and the aunt from Market Harborough, and you and me – all with our poor, diminished characters – seeking for ourselves and for our world a better way and the hope of glory.

THE MESSAGE OF THE MAGI

(From a sermon preached at Evensong in York Minster
on the Second Sunday after Christmas 1986.)

*There shall a star from Jacob come forth, and a sceptre from
Israel rise up.*

Numbers 24: 17

These words of the anthem* which we have just heard are
taken from Balaam's prophecy as recorded in the Book of
Numbers. Balaam the prophet had been hired by Balak, King
of Moab, to curse Balak's enemies, the Israelites. That is why
Balak kept the prophet – to curse his enemies and to secure
divine protection for his nation. Balaam, however, refused. To
the dismay of his employer the prophet pronounced a blessing
upon the people of Israel instead of a curse, and foretold the
defeat of Moab. 'There shall a star from Jacob come forth,' he
said.

And for us, that star has indeed risen. Tomorrow is the
Feast of the Epiphany: the Church will celebrate the rising of
the Light of Christ upon the nations.

One of the stories read at the Epiphany tells us of the Wise
Men from the East. Associated with that story are a cluster
of biblical texts, of which this evening's first lesson (Isaiah
60: 1–9), with its reference to camels and gifts of gold and

---

* The anthem sung by the choir was 'There shall a star from Jacob come forth' by Felix
Mendelssohn.

21

frankincense, was one. The text of the anthem was another. The Wise Men or Magi were members of an Eastern sect and their story is a timely reminder to the Church that Christ cannot be confined to Christianity; that the truth of God manifest in Jesus is a truth which can be approached not only along the single path of traditional Christian doctrine, but along many less obvious routes. That is part of the meaning of the story of the Magi.

This should not surprise us. The opening verses of the Gospel according to St John – words familiar to us from the carol service – tell us that Christ 'is the true light which lighteth every man that cometh into the world'. It is no wonder, then, that such a light should be found reflected in the minds and actions of men and women who would never call themselves Christian.

The Feast of the Epiphany reminds the Church of something else. The story of Christmas is painted on a small canvas: the picture of the stable and the manger, of Joseph, Mary and the shepherds is held in a narrow frame, but the visit of the Wise Men and the manifestation of God's glory to the wisdom of the Orient interprets the nativity of Christ on a cosmic scale. The canvas, large enough to accommodate the cosmic movement of the stars, is no less than Creation itself, the frame no narrower than the universe.

When they saw his star, they rejoiced with exceeding great joy. When they came to Bethlehem they were filled with wonder to find how that cosmic event could be reduced to the domestic scale of a mother and her child.

As we move from Christmas to Epiphany we pray that in following the star of Bethlehem we neither lose sight of the cosmic grandeur of God's incarnation, nor forget the domestic simplicity of his birth.

A SONG OF CREATION

(From a sermon preached at Matins in Withyham Parish Church
on Septuagesima Sunday 2009.)

Solomon Grundy
Born on a Monday
Christened on Tuesday
Married on Wednesday
Ill on Thursday
Worse on Friday
Died on Saturday
Buried on Sunday
And that is the end of Solomon Grundy.

It is no accident that this nursery rhyme compresses life into a week. The period of seven days – that basic span by which Western culture measures time – is of ancient origin. It is hard-wired into our consciousness. So much so that we hardly notice it. So familiar is it to our daily lives that it is hard to imagine existence without the seven-day cycle: Sunday, Monday, Tuesday, Wednesday, Thursday, Friday, Saturday.

Scholars believe that the notion of the seven-day week, which frames the Song of Creation* in the Bible, was borrowed from the ancient Babylonians. The week later became fundamental to Jewish tradition: six days of work followed by a day of rest, the Sabbath. The Christian tradition turned

---

* Genesis 1: 1–2: 3.

this sequence around; we celebrate the first day of the week: Sunday, the day of Christ's resurrection. But the seven-day shape remains and is fundamental to the sacred calendars of Judaism, Christianity and Islam, as well as to the commercial, diplomatic and political calendars of the Western world.

The opening verses of the Book of Genesis have been called a Song of Creation. It is our earliest celebration of the week. The repetition of certain phrases, like 'and the evening and the morning were the first day'... or second day... and so on, and the chorus 'God saw that it was good', are the refrains of an ancient Hebrew poem which scholars believe is based upon an even more ancient rhythmic chant, originating in one of the tribal cultures from which the Hebrew people sprang.

What is the poem all about, and why should we hear it recited in church, as we have done today? Well, it is a poem celebrating the three great truths which run through the Bible, and which are fundamental not only to our religion, but indeed to much of Western philosophy.

These are the three truths:

That the whole universe belongs to a single scheme of existence.

That this huge enterprise is fundamentally good – that is, 'fit for purpose'.

That humanity has a special duty to care for the environment.

The coherence of our universe is something we now take for granted. Of course creation holds together, you might say. After all, that is what the word 'universe' means. But at one time there was no 'of course' about it. There were many beliefs which depicted life on this planet as a series of continuous conflicts between mysterious powers – a meaningless and frightening confusion inherent in creation itself.

The Song of Creation in Genesis opposes the theory of confusion with the belief that underlying all life and sustaining the entire universe is the principle of Order. The supremacy of order over chaos is expressed in the opening verses of the poem in the metaphor of God's Spirit, or breath, moving over the face of the waters – the dark waters of chaos – and then using a second image (an image which recurs throughout the Bible) of God's Word, his utterance (a development of the image of breath), literally speaking order into existence: 'Let there be light... Let there be a firmament... Let dry land appear... Let there be animals...' and so on. The divine *Fiat*.

The second of the three truths expressed in the Song of Creation is the underlying goodness of Creation. The poem reiterates 'and God saw that it was good'. This belief – again fundamental to the Bible – is one which underlies our contemporary reverence for the fragility of the ecology. Zoologists (like Darwin) and botanists testify to their wonder at the miraculous abundance of animal and plant life. Physicists talk of their awe as they peer into the materials of existence.

And the third truth expressed in this poem (that humanity has been given stewardship for the environment – for its preservation and, where appropriate, its management) is one now acknowledged by all civilised societies in the world. Running through the Bible is the message that we must treat the natural order with reverence because it is God's creation... and not to exploit or destroy it.

These three great truths: the coherence of creation, the goodness of the natural order, and humanity's duty of care, are expressed in the first chapter of Genesis – they are truths which scientists and theologians hold in common – truths which move us, whatever our religious beliefs, to respond with wonder and reverence to creation.

LENT: A TIME FOR SELF-ASSESSMENT

(From a Lent Address given at St Alban's,
Wood Street Village, Guildford, on 10 March 2004.)

We need to change. I need to change. You need to change. Not at the superficial level of manners, attitude or opinion; not how we do things or behave. But how we see ourselves. How we esteem our lives.

Esteem. Now, there's an interesting word. It comes from the Latin meaning copper. To esteem was to calculate a thing's cash value: how many copper coins is it worth in the market? Jesus spoke about sparrows being sold at five for two pennies, and yet, he assures us, not one of them is forgotten in the sight of God.

Here are two scales of estimation: the cash value at the market stall, which fluctuates according to supply and demand, and the true, intrinsic and permanent value of a sparrow in the eyes of her creator. We may consider ourselves to be worth more than a tree-full of sparrows, but even our own self-assessment does not amount to much in the world's marketplace. Our Lord assures us, however, that you and I are infinitely precious in the estimation of our heavenly Father.

Jean Vanier, the Canadian theologian and founder of *L'Arche*, an international organisation which runs communities for people with serious disabilities, wrote of a chilling encounter he had with a man convicted of multiple murders. Vanier wrote,* 'He was like a block of ice; vibrations of hate seemed to flow from him... I remember a terrible feeling of

---

* *Finding Peace*, Jean Vanier 2003.

unease I experienced as I stood in his presence. Yet I could almost read his history. Around his heart he must have built up layer and layer of barriers to protect himself. He had been unwanted as a child, emotionally and physically abused. If he had always been treated as a thing to be used or controlled and never as a person, how could he trust anyone? How could he trust himself? How could he change?'

Low self-esteem makes sinners of us all. Only love can break through our barriers and restore our self-esteem. Love, and its distant cousin, Good Manners.

Candida Lycett Green wrote of her father John Betjeman, 'His great gift to anyone who came into contact with him was to talk about *them,* to bring them from the shadows into to the limelight, however briefly, and leave them with a feeling of self-worth.'

Zacchaeus, the dishonest tax-collector in Jericho – his story is in Luke 19:1–10 – was trapped in his little world of fraud. Years of habit and years of public scorn had driven him to hide behind his barricade. One day he climbed into a sycamore tree from which to observe the miracle-worker of Galilee – to see, but not to be seen. But he was rumbled and, for once they didn't laugh at the ridiculous little fellow. 'Zacchaeus,' said Jesus, 'hurry and come down; I must stay at your house today.'

Love spoke the word, and Zacchaeus was set free. Liberated, he could now begin to change.

You and I are called by Christ to change. Not to change our routines, but to change how we see ourselves, how we esteem ourselves. We are worth so much more than tuppence. None of us and none of this world's rogues and villains is less than infinitely precious in the sight of God.

Lent is a time for self-assessment, a time to open our eyes and see exactly who we are: beloved children of our heavenly Father. Accept that, and everything else begins to make sense.

GUILDFORD'S *VIA DOLOROSA*

(From a sermon preached at Holy Trinity Church, Guildford, on Palm Sunday 1999. These words followed an enactment of the Passion narrative, which told of the Last Supper, Trial and Crucifixion of our Lord.)

It was such a public way of dying. Such a waste of a young life. We have been there this morning. We have seen enacted before us the whole story. We have followed the victim on the way to his place of death. We have walked the street to Golgotha. The Street of Sorrow. The *Via Dolorosa*. We have gone back 2,000 years to Jerusalem.

But we do not need to go further than Guildford to find Christ's *Via Dolorosa*. We do not need to go back 2,000 years to see his crucifixion.

Two weeks ago I was walking back from the post office in North Street. It was a beautiful sunny day, and the crowd of shoppers were bustling, happy, carefree. Spring was in the air. As I walked down Haydon Place a group of noisy, laughing, jostling youngsters carrying guitars approached from the direction of the Academy of Contemporary Music. When they were still some way off, I saw them stop all of a sudden and fall silent. One of them was pointing at something which had been propped against the wall. After a few moments they moved on, but now they were quiet and thoughtful.

When I got to the place, I saw what they had seen. A spray of flowers and a piece of paper on which was written: 'Sally died here 10 March 1999 RIP'. Next to this lay her blanket, neatly folded.

We read about Sally in the *Surrey Advertiser*: how she had been living rough; how she had sunk through a spiral of neglect, alcohol and drugs, until her body was so weakened that in that frosty night not even the warm air from the ventilator grill over which she used to huddle could save her.

It was such a public way of dying. Such a waste of a young life. For Sally her *Via Dolorosa* was here in Guildford. For Jesus it was in Jerusalem. Two young people. Two victims. Two outcasts. Two deaths. We celebrate one as a victory, and over the other we shake our heads and call it a tragic waste.

But is it not our Christian faith that God sees beyond the waste, the failure, the squalor; that our Lord recognises himself in every life however flawed, however fragmented; that he saw himself in Sally as she died an outcast's death, alone, on a pavement in Guildford two weeks ago?

I hope so. I really hope so. Otherwise, what will become of us all?

O Saviour of the world,
Who by your Cross and precious blood have redeemed us,
Save us and help us, we humbly beseech you, O Lord. Amen.

THE ROYAL MAUNDY

24 March 2016

A friend of mine, and fellow priest, was one of the 180 recipients of the Royal Maundy in 2016. He invited me to be his companion for the occasion, which took place in St George's Chapel, Windsor.

'Maundy' derives from the Latin 'mandatum' (commandment) and refers to the occasion at the Last Supper when Jesus girded himself with a towel and washed his disciples' feet as a sign of humility and service. He said, 'I give you a new commandment that you love one another.' In the Middle Ages the sovereign or his deputy would wash the feet of a selected group of paupers and make gifts of clothing and food. In 1501, for example, Henry VII's queen, Elizabeth, used warm water scented with flowers for the ceremony of the *pedilavium* (foot-washing).

Kings and queens were not the only people to observe the custom. Cardinal Wolsey did so in 1530, as recorded by his biographer, George Cavendish: 'Upon Maundy Thursday he made his Maundy in our Lady's Chapel [in Peterborough Abbey] having fifty-nine poor men, whose feet he washed, wiped and kissed; each of these poor men had twelve pence in money, three ells of canvass to make them shirts, a pair of new shoes, a cast of bread, three red herrings, and three white herrings, and the odd person had two shillings.'* Cavendish

---

★　*Thomas Wolsey, His Life and Death of George Cavendish*, ed. Roger Lockyer. Folio Society 1962.

does not explain what he means by 'the odd person'.

By the time of Charles I a degree of detachment had crept in. At the Royal Maundy at Whitehall Palace in 1633, the King observed, while the Lord High Almoner and his chaplain officiated. As each recipient lifted his foot it was held by the Almoner, who then carefully kissed his own thumb to avoid direct contact. James II was the last sovereign to wash the feet of the poor in person.

At some point in the Middle Ages there arose the custom of matching the number of recipients to the age of the giver. Wolsey was in his fifty-ninth year when he made his Maundy at Peterborough. Queen Elizabeth II was in her ninetieth year in 2016 and so the recipients numbered ninety men and ninety women – the largest number ever. By contrast the smallest number of recipients was recorded in 1423 when her ancestor, the infant Henry VI, presented two pairs of shoes and two gowns of russet cloth. Towels of Flanders linen were provided for the foot-washing of the two paupers.

In modern times foot-washing has been dropped from the Royal Maundy, and token gifts are presented to pensioners in recognition of their service to church and community. The gifts of cloth and shoes have been replaced by purses of money. Recipients are now each given two purses: a red one holding money in lieu of food and clothing, and a white one containing the four Maundy coins, specially minted in silver.

The ceremony on 24 March 2016 was due to start at 11am. Before then, however, there were several formal entrances, the first being that of the Yeomen of the Guard, splendid in their Tudor bonnets and scarlet and yellow coats. They each carried a halberd – a nine-foot-long pole, surmounted by a sharp spearhead with which to inflict lethal injury upon anyone threatening harm to the sovereign. There must have been a score or so of these grizzled janissaries, slow-marching round the chapel and looking as if they meant business. Their approach, as they came towards us down the north aisle, was signalled by a loud thumping sound as their leader struck the floor with the butt of his halberd at each stride. As their procession slow marched round the chapel, some of them peeled off to mount guard at strategic positions.

Other processions included that of the Military Knights – a small company of ancient warriors originally formed in 1348, two years after the Battle of Crecy, when King Edward III provided lodging for twenty-six veterans of the war with France. In return for shelter and sustenance, the 'poor knights' undertook to pray daily for their sovereign and for the members of the Order of the Garter. Today's Military Knights of Windsor attend the sovereign on state occasions in St George's Chapel, where they bear their office with grave panache.

Behind the Military Knights came 'The Children and Gentlemen of Her Majesty's Chapel Royal'. This choir, numbering ten boys and six men, has been present at royal occasions down the centuries. It was there to sing Mass on the eve of Agincourt in 1415, and it was there, too, at the Field of Cloth of Gold to accompany King Henry VIII when he met the French King Francis I, and the two monarchs vied with each other in royal splendour.

At 11am precisely the sovereign made her entrance. She and Prince Philip arrived at the north entrance and came down the full length of the north aisle, then up the central aisle to their seats placed to the west of the screen, thus giving us all a close view as they passed by. She wore a conspicuous blue hat, thus enabling those at a distance at least to see her hat moving along between the shoulders of the crowd.

Then followed the service itself. It consisted of two Bible readings, anthems and prayers, cast in a sixteenth-century style of formal English reminiscent of the Book of Common Prayer.

The Queen made the distribution in two perambulations, first walking down the chapel along the rows of recipients on the south side and then returning to her seat for the second reading, before setting off again to make her presentations to those on the north side. For someone of her age it was an astonishing display of self-discipline, concentration and energy. She did not falter or hesitate. Her manner was unhurried, and yet if you were to time the event you would be surprised how quickly she moved.

And here was her achievement: she made every one of those 180 pensioners experience an individual, personal and unforgettable encounter with their sovereign as she thanked them for their public service.

THE FEAST OF THE ASCENSION

(From a sermon preached at Withyham Parish Church
on the Sunday after Ascension Day 2006.)

The Christian religion is a mixture of natural and supernatural. Or, put another way, the Gospel is a story of events which can be measured by the usual tests of historical truth – tests which ask. 'What happened?', 'When did it happen?', 'Who saw it happen?' In that sense it is part of the natural order of this world. But it is also a narrative intersected by events which lie outside the natural order.

When we hear the story about Christ's trial before Pontius Pilate and his crucifixion we are being presented with historical events which can be measured by the same criteria as other contemporary events like, for example, the British leader Boudicca's revolt against the Roman legions or the volcanic eruption of Vesuvius and the destruction of Pompeii. The life of Jesus Christ, his teaching, arrest, trial and death, belong to the same continuum of time and space as the rest of recorded history.

But the story presented in the New Testament makes a greater claim. It affirms that in Christ an altogether different continuum intersects that of time and space. To know Christ we need more than the evidence of history, otherwise he remains a distant figure from a bygone age.

If I show you a picture of some famous historical figure and ask you to tell me about him or her, you will give me an account of that person according to the facts insofar as you know them. But if I show you a picture of someone very well known to you, perhaps a close friend or a member of your family, and ask you to tell me what you know about him or her, you will give me so much more than the historical facts. The facts will be there, of course, but you will find it impossible to detach those facts from your own feelings about that person. Unavoidably your own relationship with that person will colour your account.

What we have in the New Testament is a portrait, or rather, a number of portraits coloured by the disciples' own response to the Jesus they had known in Galilee and Jerusalem. These portraits were not photographs. They were the impressionistic compositions of people's memories. They recorded much more than the bare facts.

And what was their overriding feeling and response to those facts? What so moved those disciples that they wanted to tell us, and went to such risk to themselves, even facing martyrdom, to tell us? It was their conviction that in the person of Christ they had met such a transforming power of love, of healing, of peace and of joy that they described the encounter as God himself acting in their lives.

And so for them the facts of Christ's life were edged with the flame of their own passionate faith and trust in him. Nowhere does this flame burn more brilliantly than in their account of the Ascension of their Lord.

The facts, as recorded by Luke in the last chapter of his Gospel, and more fully in the first chapter of his account of the Acts of the Apostles, are spare:

> *Then he led them out as far as Bethany, and, lifting up his hands, he blessed them. While he was blessing them, he withdrew from them and was carried up into heaven. And they worshipped him, and returned to Jerusalem with great joy; and they were continually in the temple blessing God.*

It is a brief account, short on detail, but big on impact. There are two very important details: St Luke tells us that the disciples then returned to Jerusalem *with great joy.* Hardly the reaction you would expect of people who had just said goodbye. But this was a story told by people who had come to understand that Christ's departure from their sight – the removal of his physical presence – was the beginning of a new, spiritual and therefore more real presence amongst them. His departure was an arrival.

And the cloud, a potent symbol in Jewish tradition of the glory of God – the same cloud that had descended on Mount Sinai and had enveloped Moses, the same cloud which had descended upon Jesus on the Mount of the Transfiguration – that cloud was, for the disciples, an unambiguous statement that God was in Christ, and Christ in God. This was not the end: it was the beginning. When, years after the event, the disciples came to put into writing what they had encountered that day on the Mount of Olives, they may have been uncertain of the detail, but two things they knew. Of two things they were sure: the Glory of God in Christ, and his continuing presence in their lives.

The disciples were sure of that and rejoiced. And Christians down the ages, too, have been sure of it: Christians like Charles Wesley, whose words we often sing:

Rejoice, the Lord is King
Your Lord and King adore
Mortals give thanks and sing
And triumph evermore
Lift up your heart, lift up your voice
Rejoice, again I say, rejoice!

SILENT WITNESS

(First published in the *Church Times* 21 June 2019,
in celebration of the feast of Corpus Christi.)

In the morning I say, 'Blessed are you, Sovereign God, creator of all: to you be glory and praise forever.' But I say it silently, not aloud. Although I believe that the truth those words express is fundamental to my life, I do not shout them from the rooftop. Why not? Am I a coward, afraid to acknowledge in public my Lord Jesus Christ? Even those four words – 'My Lord Jesus Christ' – I find hard to say in ordinary conversation, unless I speak them within the context of a church service – within, that is, the *cordon sanitaire* of my profession. My clerical collar licenses me to speak the unspeakable.

Even if I had the courage, as some do, to stand on the street corner and proclaim, 'I have found the answer to life's riddle and its pain. I have seen a glory that transfigures all,' I would not do so.

English reserve has been blamed for our reluctance to speak of the eternal verities. We are ready at the dinner table to utter our opinion of the current performance of England's cricket team or the new production of *Parsifal* at Covent Garden or the latest TV psycho-drama (plot inscrutable, diction inaudible, camera angles all over the place), but we are reduced to a shocked silence by a fellow guest's tactless reference to our Christian belief. Is there more than good manners to account for our embarrassment?

Lord Melbourne, that quintessential English gentleman, was uneasy when quizzed by the young Queen over his noticeable absence from church. He claimed he was 'afraid to go for fear of hearing something very extraordinary'. She was not convinced by his affected flippancy, and said so. Disraeli, the young outsider, observed Melbourne's uneasy behaviour at the Coronation when he wore his coronet deliberately askew and carried the great Sword of State 'like a butcher'. Likewise, friends of the bride-groom affect a detached amusement at the solemn proceedings, lest they be seen to take them too seriously.

But there is more to our embarrassment than diffidence. There is a deeper cause. In 1905 the young T S Eliot asked the 'overwhelming question' in his poem 'The Love Song of J Alfred Prufrock'. It is the question many of us feel but cannot find the words to utter.

Prufrock, the weary cynic, invites us to go with him through half-deserted streets, the arid townscape of our lives, the emptiness and disappointments, the failed hopes and lost vision, the bonhomie and vapid hilarity, and at every turn the crushing triviality of it all – a life measured out in coffee spoons. He wonders whether, even if he had the courage to challenge life, it would have been worth the bother. What would be the point were he:

To have squeezed the universe into a ball
To roll it toward some overwhelming question,
To say: 'I am Lazarus, come from the dead,
Come back to tell you all, I shall tell you all' –

Why put the question if the hearer were to reply, 'That's not what I meant. That's not it, at all.'

Like many who have read that poem, and possibly like the poet himself, I too have been Prufrock, unable to communicate not the doubting question, 'What is it?', but the glorious answer. Perhaps it were better to remain a silent witness than to speak out and then be misunderstood.

We lack a language to express our deepest thoughts and are accustomed to making do with the loose change of small talk. Ready-made phrases, colloquial asides, conventional half-truths provide us with a ready currency. Irony, not solemnity, is our default position in society. We are at a loss when serious issues call for a rarer coinage.

Did Lazarus tell them all? Did he proclaim, 'I have found the answer to life's riddle and its pain. I have seen a glory that transfigures all'? Perhaps at first he did, but as the months passed and the daily routines reasserted themselves, life in Bethany must have returned to normal. Neighbours soon got used to seeing him round the village, every morning waiting to catch the bus to work and in the evening digging his allotment.

And when they met his sister, Martha, at the corner shop, bustling as usual, this time to buy some tea for her friend from Galilee who had dropped in unexpectedly, they talked about this and that, but with only a fleeting reference to Lazarus – 'Your brother all right now, dear?' – before reverting to the price of sugar.

What their friend from Galilee later gave Lazarus and his sisters was indeed the answer to life's riddle and its pain. At first, when he said, 'I am the resurrection and the life,' they did not understand. But later they did, when they saw Christ's glory shining from the Cross transfiguring all. He gave them, as he gives us too, a language strong enough to bear the weight of that reality. 'This is my Body which is given for you... This is my Blood which is shed for you,' are for us the Words of Life, to be spoken quietly, not shouted from the rooftop or proclaimed at the street corner or headlined in bold or diminished to a strapline, but uttered and received within the quiet intimacy of a holy communion.

TOO COMPLEX TO BE A MARTYR:

TOO HONEST TO BE A COWARD

Thomas Cranmer
1489–1556

A contemporary wrote of Thomas Cranmer:

He was a man of such temperature of nature... that no manner
of prosperity or adversity could alter or change his accustomed
conditions. To the face of the world his countenance... never
altered. Notwithstanding privately with his secret and special
friends he would shed forth many bitter tears, lamenting the
misery and calamities of the world.

(Ralph Morice)

He was born in 1489 into a family of Nottinghamshire gentry.
He was educated at Jesus College, Cambridge where he was
elected a Fellow and was ordained in 1523. An active supporter of
Henry VIII's divorce from Queen Catherine, he was appointed
ambassador to the Emperor Charles V, and in 1531 Archbishop
of Canterbury. Under the Protestant regime of Edward VI he
compiled the First and Second Books of Common Prayer in 1549
and 1552. Under Mary Tudor he was tried for heresy and burnt at
the stake in 1556. As part of the Elizabethan Settlement his Prayer
Book (later revised in 1662) became one of the foundation texts
of the Church of England. The Church commemorates him on
the day of his martyrdom, 21 March.

He was, as they say, a private man; not a born leader, nor
a natural martyr. But we would be quite wrong to think that

he lacked passion. He married twice and on each occasion impetuously, risking his career. As Diarmaid MacCulloch wrote (*Thomas Cranmer*, 1996), he 'was clearly the marrying kind'. His first love was Joan, for whom he lost his college Fellowship and his job. She died young in childbirth. About a dozen years later, just as his career at court was taking off – the King had sent him on an embassy to the Emperor Charles V – he fell in love with Margarete, niece by marriage of the Lutheran reformer Andreas Osiander. Their marriage in Nuremberg was in breach of his clerical vow of celibacy and had to be kept hidden. Despite this, it lasted until his death twenty-four years later.

His well-known public career was shaped by the shifting demands of Tudor politics, vacillating between Catholic and Protestant. His detractors saw him as inconstant, weak. Those who knew him best recognised an inner honesty. His generation of reformers had, after all, been nurtured in the piety and practice of the Catholic Church. They were brought up as Catholics. They were pathfinders, uncertain where reform would lead.

Francisco de Quiñones, the Spanish cardinal, introduced his revised breviary of 1536 with the statement (in Latin): 'There was never anything by the wit of man so well devised, or so sure established, which, in continuance of time might not be improved.' Cranmer began his preface to the 1549 Prayer Book with the same words in English but replaced the last sentence with the words 'which in continuance of time hath not been corrupted'. It was a question of emphasis. In fact, Cranmer owed much to the Catholic revisionist, as well as to the Lutheran reformers. His genius as a liturgist lay in his deft use of existing texts. There is very little in the Prayer Book which does not have its source in the pre-Reformation breviary, missal and primers, the very texts which Cranmer, Latimer and Ridley would have learnt as young priests and would have continued to use for most of their lives.

He had a gentle touch, often softening and enriching the terse diction of the Latin liturgy. For example, his translation of the collect for Easter 4 (transferred to the Third Sunday before Lent in *Common Worship*) is expanded in English to twice its original length. The rather stark opening '*Deus, qui fidelium mentes unius efficis voluntatis*' becomes the more gracious 'O Almighty God, who alone canst order the unruly wills and affections of sinful men'. To the ancient marriage vow, cast in the language of a binding contract ('to have and to hold, from this day forward, for better for worse, for richer for poorer, in sickness and in health') Cranmer added the phrase 'to love and to cherish', offering the couple a prospect so much more delightful than a bare *quid pro quo*. He also included in the marriage service a reference to 'the mutual society, help and comfort that the one ought to have of the other'. No doubt he was thinking about his own marriage to Margarete.

After Edward VI's premature death Cranmer endorsed the succession, legitimised by the late King's will, of Lady Jane Grey. He provided twenty men-at-arms to support her cause, but Princess Mary was swept to power by popular demand, and Queen Jane executed as a traitor. It was Cranmer's downfall. In his last letter smuggled out of prison to Peter Martyr, he wrote, 'I pray that God may grant that we may endure to the end,' but this was not to be. His trial and imprisonment broke his spirit. He recanted, and signed papers submitting to the Pope. Then, appalled, he withdrew his recantation. In the end this elderly man, too complex to be a martyr, too honest to be a coward, was hurried through the streets of Oxford to die a horrible and heroic death.

EMBROIDERY SPEAKS WITH MANY VOICES

(From the Broderers' Service held in the Chapel of St Nicholas
in York Minster on 22 June 1983 to dedicate a new set of
embroidered kneelers. Their theme was 'The Twelve Days of
Christmas'. The following words, written for the occasion,
were spoken by the Dean during the service of dedication.)

Embroidery speaks in many voices. Its message is at once
simple and elaborate, direct and oblique. It can tell the great
truths of the Christian faith in symbols of Chalice and Cross
and Crown. Thereby it illuminates our public utterance of
creed and praise. But it can also speak in the vernacular of
folklore, decorating with the flourish and curlicue of legend
the margins of our belief.

Sometimes it speaks an intimate language which, though
elusive, is accessible to all. When overcome by the splendour
of transepts and nave, the visitor to the Minster can find
peace in St Stephen's Chapel or All Saints', and catch there
the meaning of those flowers and crowns, and marvel at this
quiet disclosure of grace beneath the trumpeting columns of
the great gothic choir.

Embroidery speaks also in a woman's voice, using the
needle of irony to prick the bubble of male conceit. Those
emblems and trophies of military pride, lovingly stitched by
regimental wives, do not intend to celebrate the old delusions
of war. Rather, they record with painful clarity the courage of
husbands and sons spent in the grim waste of man's unending
strife.

The tone of irony is most sharply heard in this: that in a
chapel which rings with the echoes of England's wars with

France, where the symbols of masculine aggression are all around, it is a woman's dress which furnishes the altar – and she a member of the French King's court.*

Lest we should become too serious, the language of embroidery employs its wit to deflate religious pomp. In the Minster's Zouche Chapel the plump jenny-wren forever poised to catch her spider and here eight maids a-milking and ten lords a-leaping remind us that there is sometimes more truth in nonsense than in all our pious homilies.

And so in this place where many voices join the angels and archangels in their ceaseless song of praise, and where above our heads the chorus of stone and glass resounds through transept, nave and choir, closer at hand, audible but not intrusive, is a quieter voice whose art is to embellish, to inform, to modify and to delight.

---

* The dossal curtain of green and gold silk brocade, which hangs behind the altar of St John's Chapel, was fashioned from an eighteenth-century dress of a member of Louis XV's court at Versailles. In its chinoiserie design recur vignettes of a lady fishing with rod and line – she has just caught a large fish – and a youth sitting beside a flowing stream in a pastoral landscape. It was presented to the Minster by the regiment of the King's Own Yorkshire Light Infantry, the names of whose men, killed in the Peninsular campaign against Napoleon, are recorded on a mural tablet. Also in the chapel is a bust of Sir John Moore who died of his wounds at Corunna. The kneelers in the chapel were worked by wives of the regiment.

LES DAMES DU TEMPS JADIS

Dictes moy où, n'en quel pays,
Est Flora, la belle Romaine;
Archipiada, ne Thaïs,
Qui fut sa cousine germaine;
Echo, parlant quand bruyt on maine
Dessus rivière ou sus estan,
Qui beauté eut trop plus qu'humaine?
Mais où sont les neiges d'antan!

François Villon, c1431–63

François Villon's *Ballade des dames du temps jadis*, or at least, its
final line, is a familiar lament on the lips of old age. Where,
indeed, have they all gone, those brave women of yesterday?
Où sont les neiges d'antan? Like last year's snows they have
melted away. In his four-verse ballad the poet lists the heroic
names of the past, amongst them Flora and Thaïs, Blanche of
Castile, Abelard's doomed lover Héloise, and the courageous
Joan of Arc.

Miss Sheen was cast in that same heroic mould. Not as a
doomed lover, nor as her nation's martyr but as someone who,
like those legendary *dames du temps jadis*, had risen majestically
above life's cruel circumstances. She cut a noble figure as she
glided round the dance floor, demonstrating to us, her young
pupils, the waltz, the foxtrot and the military two-step.

Ballroom dancing at my preparatory school was an 'extra',
like carpentry and drawing. Miss Sheen taught us to regard
ourselves as an elite corps of young gentlemen, a privileged
few, set apart from the ruck of rude little boys with their

pushing and shoving, their coarse jokes, conkers and marbles. She was kind but firm, and carried about her the grand manner of a former age.

'Don't just leave him there, Leak,' she would boom at me as I broke away from my partner at the conclusion of a stumbling caper round the floor. 'There's no need to forget your manners, just because it's a *rumba*.' She made no secret of her disapproval of Latin American rhythms, but felt compelled to include them in our education; it was, after all, 1948.

As directed, I would reluctantly conduct my partner, Linforth, back to his seat and, bowing deeply as we were taught to do, I would thank him for the pleasure of the dance. 'Next time, it's *my* turn to lead,' he muttered.

The manners Miss Sheen taught us were those which would have prevailed at an Edwardian *thé-dansant*, but the music being thumped out relentlessly by a jobbing pianist on a broken keyboard was straight from the repertoire of a 1948 saloon bar. We sensed, even at our young age, the discrepancy between a world in which young gentlemen wore white gloves at dances and the music, which on this occasion was a popular melody about the rich Maharajah of Magador who had 'rubies and pearls, and the loveliest girls, but didn't know how to do-oo the rumba'.

It was many years later that I learnt the truth about Miss Sheen. For professional purposes she used her maiden name. In fact, she was a young war widow. Trained for the ballet in the 1930s, she had been afflicted by some kind of glandular imbalance during adolescence, which had accelerated her growth both upwards and outwards, compelling her to give up her chosen career. Marriage during the war to a young army officer was a brief happiness: he was killed on the Normandy beaches. Thereafter, her life was tied to the treadmill of the prep school circuit, scrimping enough money to pay the rent for her smart service flat in Marylebone, where a signed picture of Claudio Arrau held pride of place on her Steinway grand and invitation cards from her wealthy friends gathered on the mantle-piece.

Hers was by no means a rare situation. She was one of so many young women having to make do without husbands in those bleak post-war winters of power cuts and rationing. Even now, seventy years later, I can remember them, those bereaved mothers of my friends, battling through the wind and rain from the railway station at Westgate-on-Sea to take their sons out after chapel on a Sunday morning. Of the eight contemporaries who began their boarding school careers with me in the summer term of 1946, four had lost their fathers in the war. That proportion, if replicated across the nation, was a terrible statistic of broken lives, but at the time we children did not know the price the mothers had to pay.

All those brave women, *ces dames du temps jadis*, called to live lives so very different from their pre-war dreams: they were heroic in their endurance. They just got on with life and struggled single-handedly to bring up their children in the post-war years. Remarriage? Who would want to take on a woman with two or three young children at heel?

And where are they now, those valiant hearts? For a while they carried on, but playing a diminishing role in the lives of their growing sons and daughters. As the years passed so their importance declined. They found themselves pushed ever so gently to the wings as succeeding generations now moved centre-stage; first their children, then their grandchildren and now their great-grandchildren.

Où sont les neiges d'antan?

FATHER OF THE ENGLISH REFORMATION

William Tyndale
1491–1536
Translator of the Bible

(First published in the *Church Times* October 2017.)

'I wish that the husbandman may sing parts of [the Scriptures] at his plough, that the weaver may warble them at his shuttle, and that the traveller may with their narratives beguile the weariness of the way,' wrote Erasmus in the preface to his 1516 edition of the Greek New Testament. A few years later Luther and Tyndale used Erasmus's Greek New Testament to make this dream possible for German and English-speaking readers.

The availability of the Bible in the vernacular and the invention of the printing press were the two engines of the Reformation. To them must be added the expansion in the early sixteenth century of trade between the countries of northern Europe and the growth of the mercantile class as it supplanted the clergy and the landed aristocracy in power and influence.

Tyndale had strong family connections with London's city merchants. It was to them he turned as a young man when he knew that his reformist views made him *persona non grata* with Cuthbert Tunstall, the Bishop of London. He found refuge in the Steelyard – an enclosed collection of Thames-side quays, warehouses, chapel and accommodation belonging to London merchants trading with the Hanseatic ports in the Low Countries and Germany.

Throughout his twenty-two years' exile on the continent he made much use of these contacts and was sometimes funded by them. It was in their ships that Tyndale's bibles were smuggled into England. When he was finally arrested in Antwerp he had been living under the protection of the 'English House', the residence belonging to English merchants trading in Flanders and Germany.

Tyndale's New Testament was not the first to appear in English. More than a century earlier Wycliffe and his followers had produced a translation into the vernacular. What was new was that the Wycliffites had used the Latin version (the Vulgate), but Tyndale went back to the original Greek for his translation of the New Testament and to the Hebrew for the Pentateuch. Also, he was able to use German printers and a network of trade connections by which to distribute his books.

It was a dangerous thing to do, to unlock the Scriptures from the Vulgate. The Latin straitjacket which had encased them for centuries was the foundation on which was built the entire edifice of medieval theology. Tinker with one part and the whole building might come crashing down. Erasmus knew this and was prepared to take the risk: 'I absolutely dissent from those people who do not want the holy scriptures to be read in translation by the unlearned – as if, forsooth, Christ taught such a complex doctrine that hardly anyone outside a handful of theologians could understand it.'

Thomas More, Erasmus's friend and disciple, knew it too, but he was cautious and unwilling to allow such an important matter to fall into the wrong hands. A translation might open the door to heresy.

Amongst others Cuthbert Tunstall, Bishop of London, inveighed against Tyndale's English New Testament. In 1526 he called it, 'That pestiferous and most pernicious poison dispersed throughout all our diocese of London in great number, which will contaminate and infect the flock committed unto us with most deadly poison and heresy.'

Branded as a heretic at home and abroad, Tyndale was compelled to live as a fugitive, moving under cover from Wittenberg to Cologne to Worms to Frankfurt to Antwerp, ever-vigilant of informers and ever-fleeing the long reach of Thomas More's spies. He was never safe.

Finally, Tyndale was caught. Henry VIII, who had always been ambivalent about his troublesome subject, tried to save him from execution, but Charles V, in whose jurisdiction Tyndale was held prisoner, was not willing to oblige. Tyndale was convicted of heresy and sentenced to death by strangulation at the hands of the public executioner. His martyrdom took place in Antwerp on 6 October 1536. Before he died, he was heard to cry out, 'Lord, open the King of England's eyes.'

A few months later, in 1537, the first complete English Bible was published, this time 'With the King's most gracious licence'. Known as 'Mathew's Bible', it comprised Tyndale's New Testament and Pentateuch (the first five books of the Old Testament) and the rest of the Old Testament in Coverdale's translation. In 1539 a new version, the 'Great Bible', again incorporating Tyndale's work, was ordered by Act of Parliament to be placed in every parish church. When James I's Authorised Version was published in 1611, it contained, with some revisions, Tyndale's New Testament and Pentateuch.

If any single person can be called the Father of the English Reformation, it must surely be the exiled and martyred William Tyndale.

LADY WITH A MANDOLIN

She was the wife of the last Venetian consul in Aleppo. Her portrait, painted in 1790, showed a lady of striking beauty, confident of her leading position in Levantine society. Until a few years ago the picture still hung in the same room in which it had been painted, where much of the furniture was still as she had known it. On a table near the picture was the mandolin which had been hers and which appears beside her in the painting.

Until the latter years of the twentieth century her descendants still lived in their ancestral home, the Khan Nahaseen, in the ancient copper bazaar of Aleppo. My cousin, Jenny, aged seventy-two years, was the last of the family to have known it as her home, before she gave it to the Syrian equivalent of the National Trust.

The house – a 'khan' or 'caravanserai' – was built in 1539 round a courtyard for Venetian merchants and used as their consul's residence. As was the custom, it also served as an inn for merchants, a warehouse for their merchandise and as stabling for camels and pack horses. It was the oldest continuously inhabited building in Aleppo, until it was pounded to rubble during the recent civil war. The treasures it still contained – some had already been removed to a museum – were either looted or destroyed, and its last resident, my cousin, was now no longer living, having died in 2015. Unlike so many of her neighbours she did not die from injuries sustained in war, but from an incurable illness, no doubt aggravated by the horrors of the intense bombardment and destruction of the place she loved. *'E' morta per un male incurabile tra le macerie della sua casa'* ('She died from an incurable disease in the rubble of her house') was how one newspaper reported what had happened.

Much more than a family home had perished in that heap of broken masonry. Though bad enough, that would have been no worse than what had happened in many neighbourhoods of that ancient city. Besides, the destruction of buildings, however beautiful or historic, cannot compare with the death of 23,000 civilians killed in Aleppo within the space of three years.

But here was something of a different order. The destruction of the Khan Nahaseen symbolised the end of an entire culture of interracial and interfaith cooperation between Muslim, Jew and Christian; the breaking asunder of bonds which had been formed by the mutual self-interest of trade extending back to the tenth century or earlier.

When the Venetian grandee, Lorenzo Tiepolo, took up his post as consul in 1559 and rode in procession to his residence in the Khan Nahaseen, he was accompanied by no less than two hundred and fifty Venetian merchants. He found in Aleppo a cosmopolitan city buzzing with trade. It was one of the world's great entrepôts, through which silk, cotton, gems and spices from Asia passed on their way to Europe and were exchanged for goods from Europe, including woollen fabrics, tin, lead, leather and fur, some from distant England. In Lorenzo's time the Arab *Aleppines* had established no less than five hundred looms to process imports of silk from the East.

In the sixteenth and seventeenth centuries, trading companies from Austria, France, the Netherlands, Venice and England entered treaties, known as 'capitulations', with the Ottoman Sultan. These secured rights not only to trade, but also to regulate the affairs of their expatriate communities. They formed the basis of a mercantile network across the great cities of the Eastern Mediterranean: Aleppo, Alexandria, Cairo, Smyrna, Beirut and, later, Athens.

By the beginning of the twentieth century those cities were no longer the great trading centres they had once been, but their cosmopolitan character persisted. The Levantine diaspora of European families, descended like my cousins from generations of merchants, enriched and in turn were enriched by those ancient cities of the Eastern Mediterranean with their pre-Christian and pre-Islamic roots, and their liberal culture now sadly replaced by an aggressive and sterile nationalism.

And what of my cousin's sons and daughter and their families? Like so many middle-class Syrians, they have left the country of their birth and settled in Europe or the USA.

As for the portrait of their Venetian ancestor, it was tracked down to an art dealer in Istanbul, who, when told that he was handling stolen goods, shrugged his shoulders and offered to sell it to its former owners for $20,000.

The fate of the mandolin remains unknown.

BAPTISM ADDRESS

(Sermon preached at Evensong in Guildford Cathedral,
14 January 1990. During the service Harriet Rose Rumsey
was baptised. The Dean was Officiant; the Precentor preached.)

Earlier in this service we welcomed a new member of Christ's Church. We witnessed a baptism. We saw the Dean pour water over the baby's head as he baptised her in the name of the Holy Trinity. He then made the sign of the cross on her forehead, and we all told her that she must be a courageous follower of Christ, with all that that entails. And then she was presented with a lit candle and we told her that, just as she receives light from God, she must give light to others.

It does seem a bit much: to load upon such young shoulders the full weight of religious commitment.

And so, perhaps, it is as well to remind ourselves that first and foremost baptism is a sign of liberation, and only secondarily is it a pledge of commitment. What has happened is that this little baby has been liberated from the shackles of human sinfulness, set free from the restricting influences of worldliness, released from the restraints of guilt. And all this has been done for her by God through Jesus Christ. It has been done for her as a free gift – an unconditional, no-strings-attached gift of his overwhelming love for her.

Of course, at this stage in her life she is too young to have been much bothered by the corruption of the world. In that sense she is an innocent. But in another sense, like all of us in our infancy, like any baby born into this world, she inherits a tendency to wilfulness. We are all programmed in such a way that there never was a man or woman, save one, who did not sooner or later give way to those destructive elements within – rage, malice, greed, lust and envy – and which all arise from the selfishness which is basic to our fallen condition.

Now you might think that we should not speak of such ugly things as rage and hate and greed on a joyful occasion such as a baby's christening, when all should be sweetness and light; or to speak of the harsh realities of the adult world – of envy and malice – when we have the innocence of a child before us, and when on this day at least we can leave such unpleasantness in the world outside.

But to do that – to leave the darkness of adult life out of our service – would be to mistake the purpose of baptism. Baptism is not a celebration of childhood and innocence. In fact, the sacrament of baptism really has very little to do with childhood at all.

The focus is not upon how and what the baby is today. The focus is upon her as she is and as she will be. The totality of her life; the whole span of the twenty, forty, fifty, seventy or eighty years which lie ahead. The water of baptism is poured upon her now at the start of her life, but its effect, its meaning, will operate throughout the entire duration of her existence on this earth.

Now think what this means. When we talk of the love of God, releasing her through baptism from the power of darkness we are not talking only about now, we are talking about her as she will be through all the stages of her life: as a schoolgirl, as a student, as an adult woman with a career, as someone with musical or artistic skills and, perhaps, as a wife, as a mother, as a grandmother. At every moment in her life, at every encounter, in every achievement, in every failure, in every joy, in every disappointment, she will be washed by the protective love of her redeeming Lord and released from the corruption which is, in greater or lesser measure, present in every human experience.

There is another meaning of baptism, another truth symbolised by water. In the early church, when the majority of those being baptised were adults, it was the custom, as it is still in some churches today, to submerge the candidate completely beneath the water. Sinking beneath the water and emerging again symbolised dying and rebirth. As Christians we are taught to die with Christ to our sins, and to rise again with him to a new life. Again, this is not a single, one-off experience, but a continuous process throughout our lives, and one which we shall never see complete this side of the resurrection.

And so what we have witnessed this evening is an entire human life encapsulated in one moment in time. Redeemed, purified and set free by the love of God, a love from which nothing can separate us.

May the words of St Paul become as true for this little one today as they were for him, when he wrote:

Neither death, nor life, nor angels, nor rulers, nor things present, nor things to come, nor height, nor depth, nor anything else in all creation, will be able to separate us from the love of God in Christ Jesus our Lord.

Romans 8: 38, 39

FIRST COMMUNION

(From a sermon preached at the Eucharist in York Minster
on Mid-Lent Sunday, 1986.)

It was an extraordinary event, but only three people saw it happen. What was going on? Well, you might say a parallel universe had crashed through an invisible barrier on that mountain. For a few moments – no more than that – for only a few moments those three men, Peter, James and John, found themselves transported to a different level of experience. In this world, but at the same time out of this world, before them stood Jesus, dazzlingly transfigured in glory. And then, almost before they could rub their eyes, it was over, and everything was back to normal.

'Don't tell anyone,' he said as they walked back down the mountain. 'Don't tell anyone what you saw. At least, not yet.'

We are not often given glimpses of transcendent glory. When we are, they can be unsettling and make it hard for us to climb back down the mountain and adjust to life in the foothills.

But let us think now of ten other young men: we can come back to Peter, James and John later. Among us there are ten young people who will be receiving Holy Communion for the first time. Ten of the boys in our school were confirmed on Friday – eight of them choristers, seated almost out of sight beyond the nave altar, and two of them non-choristers, sitting in your midst. And they are here this morning to make their First Communion.

What can we say to them?

What can we, who have been communicants for ten, twenty, forty, perhaps fifty years or more, say on such an important occasion in their lives? Our first words should be ones of welcome. We should make them aware – so far as is possible in the context of this formal worship – that we value them as fellow members of the Body of Christ; as children of the same heavenly Father and as inheritors with us of the Kingdom of God.

Alas, the church hasn't a very good record in this respect, though we are better than we were. One hundred and fifty years ago the Dean and Chapter, to their great credit, moved St Peter's School into its new buildings in Minster Yard. This sensible arrangement provoked the editor of the *Yorkshire Gazette* to write the following:

> *We do not exactly approve of converting the Close of a Cathedral into the site of a school. Stillness and quiet ought to reign in the vicinity of such buildings. The beautiful painted glass in the windows may be exposed to risk, and the venerable matrons who reside in the confines of Minster Yard will be in danger of being pushed or upset in their daily passage to and from the Church…*

(*Yorkshire Gazette*, 29 November 1828)

Well, as you know is so often the case, such gloomy predictions proved to be unfounded. The windows survived. As for the venerable matrons – it would have taken a lot more than a pack of noisy schoolboys to upset such determined dreadnoughts on their daily transit through the close.

However, things have improved. The Church of England now takes her younger members much more seriously, and also expects much more of them. And so our first response to the arrival of these new communicants must be one of welcome.

Our second response follows from this: if we mean what we say when we describe them as fellow members of the Body of Christ and children of the same heavenly Father, then we must acknowledge that they have as much capacity for spiritual insight as you and me. Now, to look at our sons, a number of adjectives might spring to mind, but *spiritual* would probably not be the first. Parents may find it hard to recognise their sons as spiritual people – but no harder than sons find it so to recognise their parents.

The fact is that domestic familiarity can blunt our perception of each other's spirituality. We are creatures of convention, and the conventions of family life do not encourage us to speak openly of those things which lie at the deepest level of our lives. The idiom of domestic conversation does not, on the whole, lend itself to a discussion about the presence of Jesus Christ in our lives. That's not just cowardice (though it might be partly that). It is, I believe, a healthy reticence in the face of matters which are too weighty to be expressed in the flimsy vernacular of our daily speech.

But even if by tacit consent we do not discuss with our children our faith and theirs in personal terms, we must never make the mistake of thinking that they are too young to have a faith. We must not underrate them – nor must we underrate the power of the Spirit of God to move their hearts... and to move them as deeply at the age of twelve as at the age of twenty-two or thirty-two or forty-two.

In today's Gospel we heard how Jesus was transfigured before his disciples Peter, James and John. Unexpectedly and inexplicably, the three disciples found themselves looking into the dazzling mystery of the presence of God. They were to have the same experience when they and the other disciples encountered Jesus Christ after his Resurrection.

These encounters were isolated experiences – glimpses of eternity in an otherwise mundane life; a life, like yours and mine, in which earning a living, cooking meals and paying the bills seem to take a disproportionately large part.

As a way of keeping fresh this vision of eternity, the disciples established the weekly commemoration of Christ's death and Resurrection. In the sacrament of Holy Communion, which Jesus gave them, they constructed a corporate celebration of that glimpse of heaven which they had been given.

Our regular participation in this sacrament can be for us an accommodation to the regular rhythm of our lives of those rare occasions when we too, like the disciples, have a glimpse of the dazzling mystery of the Presence of God.

How regularly our children may choose, as they grow up, to make use of the Sacrament and their membership of the church is a matter that they alone can decide. How far they will find the forms of Christian worship an effective expression of those truths which they discover at the deeper levels of their being is something which only they will come to know. But of this we parents can be certain:

That the true light that enlightens everyone who comes into the world – the Light of Christ – will shine in the lives of our sons. And that they will come to recognise his light at those levels of their being which may be hidden from us, but are revealed to our Heavenly Father, who knows each one of them and loves them to all eternity.

WEDDING ADDRESS

(Sermon preached at the wedding of Richard Benson and
Chloë D'Arcy-Orga at St Mary's Church, Quarry Street,
Guildford, on Saturday 6 September 2008.)

One of the readings you have just heard was taken from
The Song of Solomon. As you know, King Solomon was in
favour of marriage. He liked a good wedding, especially if
it was his own. You might say that when it came to the
state of holy matrimony he considered it a *good thing*. A very
good thing. In fact so good that he himself got married not
once, not twice, but again and again and again. According
to the Bible he had seven hundred wives (he later regretted
it). Richard, it would probably be as well were you not to
follow his example.

But no one can doubt the sheer joy – the reckless passion
in the words of *The Song of Solomon*. They are the words of two
young people gloriously, madly, head-over-heels in love. You
can just hear it – the rapture, the unquenchable ardour. Listen
to him as he sings:

*Arise, my love, my fair one, and come away; for now the
winter is past, the rain is over and gone. The flowers appear
on the earth; the time of singing has come, and the voice of the
turtle dove is heard in our land.*

And she says to him:

*Set me as a seal upon your heart, as a seal upon your arm; for
love is strong as death, passion fierce as the grave. Its flashes*

are flashes of fire, a raging flame. Many waters cannot quench love, neither can floods drown it.

Those are the words of two young people in love.

Shakespeare has a different take on the subject. We heard what he had to say in the second reading. He sounds a note of caution:

Let me not to the marriage of true minds
Admit impediments. Love is not love
Which alters when it alteration finds,
Or bends with the remover to remove.

He speaks of marriage as a union of true *minds*. He moves us to a higher and more enduring level. A relationship which cannot be shaken by the tempests of events or thrown off course by the squalls of temperament. Shakespeare's sonnet is the song of middle age. He himself had been married for about fifteen years when he wrote these words. He knew what he was talking about. He and his wife, Anne, had experienced the tempests and squalls of married life.

And then we come to the third reading. It is from the novel by Louis de Bernières, *Captain Corelli's Mandolin*. They are the words of an old man. Iannis is speaking to his daughter, Pelagia.

'Love,' he said, referring to breathless passion. 'Love is a temporary madness, it erupts like a volcano and then subsides.' Well, he would say that, wouldn't he? He was old. But he does go on to say:

Love is not breathlessness, it is not excitement. It is what is left over when being in love is burned away. Your roots will become so entwined that when all the pretty blossoms have fallen from your branches, you will find that you are one tree and not two.

So there we have it. Three types of loving. It is probably hard for you to imagine how your love for each other will look in middle age when you celebrate your silver wedding, and even harder when you celebrate your golden wedding in fifty years' time.

For some of us here this afternoon it is hard to recall how we felt when, long ago, we were in the grip of a reckless passion, a love whose *flashes were flashes of fire, a raging flame.*

Harder still when we look around at our fellow guests and think, 'Good heavens! Them? Whatever did she see in him?' Or, 'Whatever did he see in her?' But there can hardly be a life which has not at some point been ablaze with that raging flame. And, to be sure, there is not a love whose dying embers cannot be fanned and set aglow once more by kindness, patience and affection.

Richard and Chloë, today we, your family and friends, have come at your invitation to witness your marriage, to enter your happiness, and to stand for a while close to you and feel on our faces the glow of your love for each other. We have come with gifts to mark the occasion, but greater and more precious than anything we can give you, is what you give us: your love for each other.

A FUNERAL ADDRESS

(Sermon preached at the funeral of Henry Cornwallis Maude
in Wingham Parish Church on Friday 27 April 2018.)

*It is better to go to the house of mourning, than to go to the
house of feasting. Sorrow is better than laughter.*

Ecclesiastes 7: 1–5, 8–10

The choice of this passage which has just been read is timely.
It comes from a book whose brief chapters echo the repeated
phrase, 'Vanity of vanities, all is vanity'. It is the cry of humanity,
calling out in despair at the cruelty of fate. It is a fate which
awaits us all.

> *When the doors shall be shut in the streets* [I am quoting
> from the same book] *and all the daughters of music
> brought low… or ever the silver cord be loosed or the golden
> bowl be broken… because man goeth to his long home, and
> the mourners go about the street.*

The Bible does not spare us. It bruises us with its bleak realism.
Death is death, it says. It is an end. It leaves a gap. The gap
shocks and derails our minds.

It is not the purpose of our religion to conceal or disguise
with bland words the reality of death. Our purpose now is to
confront and to manage that reality.

There is another reality – or rather the same reality seen
from a different perspective. It is the reality of which the poet
John Donne wrote:

At the round earth's imagined corners blow
Your trumpets angels, and arise, arise
From death, you numberless infinities
Of souls.

As Christians we find in Christ the greatest reality of all. His life, his death and resurrection, these three put into correct perspective all our fears, all our doubts and all our griefs. It is our trust in him which gives us hope and enables us to endure the hard corners and sharp edges of reality.

'Grace' is a strong word. Our Lord responds to our faith by giving us his grace. A friend once challenged Henry about his belief in the goodness of God. How could he be sure? He thought for a while. At length he answered with a single word: *Grace.* It is by God's grace that we learn to endure reality.

But there is one hard edge which will continue to bruise: bereavement. The loss of a beloved husband; the loss of a father and grandfather leaves a gap which cannot be filled. Time might soften the sorrow, but the gap remains. And so it must. That unfilled gap is the measure of the love we feel for the person we have lost.

But it is our belief that the sorrows of our present life will, by the grace of God, be taken up into that greater reality which passes all understanding, when we shall at the last day stand together in the eternal presence of God and hear the words of our Lord Jesus Christ as he pronounces to all who love him,

Come ye blessed children of my Father, receive the kingdom
prepared for you from the beginning of the world.

MUSICIAN OF THE CHAPEL ROYAL

Orlando Gibbons
1583–1625

(First published in the *Church Times,* June 2012.)

Orlando Gibbons was educated at King's College, Cambridge, first as a chorister and then as an undergraduate. From 1603 until his death he was a musician of the Chapel Royal.* He was also a court musician, expert on the virginals and composer of sacred and secular music. In 1623 he was appointed organist of Westminster Abbey. Among his hymn tunes still sung are those set to 'Forth in thy name, O Lord, I go'; 'Jesu, grant me this I pray'; 'Love of the Father' and 'Drop, drop, slow tears'. He died on 5 June 1625.

Cranmer said, grudgingly, that if there was to be any church music it should be plain. No elaborate polyphony, no repetitions, but 'for every syllable a note, so that it may be sung distinctly and devoutly'. The music must not eclipse the language. Thomas Tallis, trained in the old tradition, showed what could be done in the new. His anthem 'If ye love me', is a surpassing example of Anglican choral music at its most graceful and restrained.

Sixty years later Orlando Gibbons continued the Tudor tradition. He was able to do so under the protection of King James's Chapel Royal, whilst in the parishes the organs and

---

* The term 'Chapel Royal' denotes the musical establishment, not the place where it sang.

choirs had been silenced by Puritan hostility. Among Gibbons's simpler works his anthem 'Almighty and everlasting God' (the BCP Collect for the Third Sunday after Epiphany) and the settings of the canticles for Matins and Evensong (his Short Service) match, without obscuring, the clarity and dignity of Cranmer's text.

But not all was plain and simple. Outstanding among his more florid compositions is his Ascension-tide anthem 'O clap your hands together... God is gone up with a merry noise'. Set for eight parts, it is a wonderfully rich piece, bursting with the exuberance of Psalm 47. True to the text, the musician cast off restraint in this great shout of joy. Church musicians were restricted to the text of the Bible and the liturgy, but by binding Coverdale's psalter into the Book of Common Prayer the reformers had ensured, despite themselves, that 'cheerfulness was always breaking in'. It was the language which drove the music.

Equally intense was the musical expression Gibbons gave to more reflective devotion. His tunes now associated with 'Jesu, grant me this I pray' and 'Drop, drop, slow tears', were among fourteen he had written for George Withers's *Hymns and Songs of the Church* (1623). The preface declared that the purpose of this collection of psalms and biblical paraphrases was 'To suit the common people's capacities' and that this was 'the aim of Master Orlando Gibbons in fitting them with tunes'. Vaughan Williams included eleven of those tunes in the *English Hymnal*, five of which are still sung in parish churches.

When the announcement of the betrothal of the Prince of Wales (later Charles I) to Henrietta Maria of France was celebrated at Westminster Abbey in the presence of the Court and the French ambassador, it was noted that 'the organ was touched by the best finger of the age, Mr Orlando Gibbons'. It was while he and the other members of the Chapel Royal were at Canterbury preparing for the princess's arrival at Dover that he suffered a fatal brain haemorrhage, possibly the result of an earlier injury received at the hands of a drunken lay clerk. He died aged forty-one.

Little is known about his life, apart from the bare facts. What we do have is his music, which continues to enrich our worship. Anthony à Wood, the seventeenth-century antiquary, described him as 'one of the greatest musicians and organists of his time'. Elizabeth, his widow, instructed that his epitaph should record the death of a 'most worthy husband' and father of her seven children.

A MIDDLE-AGED CHURCH

(From a sermon preached in York Minster at Matins
on Quinquagesima Sunday 1984.)

When people want to be rude about the Church of England they call her middle-aged. When they want to be very rude they call her middle-class. Leaving aside – for today – the second remark, let's have a look at the first. The Church of England is middle-aged. Is she? Well, yes, of course she is. As an institution she has been middle-aged for centuries. In fact, history hardly records a time when she was anything other than middle-aged. True, there was a time when she enjoyed her brief youth – a time of Celtic saints with strange practices and odd names and later, a time of Saxon saints with even odder names. But her salad days were brief. By the time our national institutions of monarchy and parliament emerged in the full vigour of their youth (sometime between the tenth and thirteenth century), the Church of England had already settled into sedate middle age.

And she has been middle-aged ever since. Therein lies her strength.

We are told that the disadvantage of age is that it deprives you of choice. At twenty years old the whole world lies open before you. Unencumbered by your past, you have any number of paths you can choose to take. By the time you reach forty, however, only a limited field of action is still open to you. And by the time you reach sixty it's *probably too late*. Your own history has made you the person you are, and the path you take is, to a large extent, pre-determined by your earlier choices.

Well, that may be the disadvantage of middle age. But the advantage is this: you have stopped caring.

Now it seems that this is a strong position to be in. To accept that you are limited by your past to a very narrow range of choices means that you stop trying to be good at everything and can get on with the one or two things that you know you are good at.

There are many things at which the Church of England is not at all good at. Let's face it: no good at all. There are forms of experimental ministry which are best left to the younger churches in this country – the Free Churches, both the historic dissenters as well as the many newer expressions of corporate Christianity.

There is no need to dwell on our church's shortcomings; they are obvious to all. She has usually been the first to recognise them. 'The Church of England,' said the famous headmaster of Rugby, Thomas Arnold, a hundred and fifty years ago, 'The Church of England as she now stands, no human power can save.' He was right, of course. Only divine intervention can possibly account for the continuing existence of such an institution.

But don't let us labour the obvious. Instead let's look at the one or two things which, with God's grace, she can do well. One particular skill I have in mind, and it is all part of her being middle-aged: she has learnt how to turn her potential disability – her age – into a glorious strength.

Encumbered as she is by the great weight of her ancient traditions and historic buildings, she is learning to use them to serve the needs of the present. Of course, some of the baggage from the past has had to be discarded. But not all. Nowhere is this truer than in her forms of worship. And it is in the way that she revises her liturgy that you can see her deploying, with significant scholarship, the insights of a middle-aged survivor.

The two major revisions of her liturgy – that by Cranmer in the sixteenth century and the one undertaken in our own generation – were both intentionally conservative. It was Cranmer's achievement that he plundered the past to find a liturgy for the present. Much of his Book of Common Prayer and almost all the Collects therein were translations from mediaeval Latin service books. And much the same can be said for our twentieth-century liturgy,* the real novelty of which is not to be seen in such minor details as addressing God as 'you' instead of 'thou', but in the fact that ancient forms and forgotten structures of worship have been revitalised for modern use.

That is not to say the revisions were not creative. Of course they were. But they were creative within the limits of an inherited tradition. Sir Albert Richardson, a former surveyor and architect of this cathedral, would often point out that in art there is nothing new – only a variation of something old. Because of her history it may be the vocation of the Church of England to be a continuing reminder of that truth.

Hardly an electrifying vocation, you might say, but then if she should find it altogether unexciting maybe she can draw comfort from those words of St Paul, reminding us that we are all members of the one body, and that we should not be dismayed if the part we are called to play is less spectacular than that of some other individuals or other churches.

This may be part of what St Paul meant when he wrote: 'For just as the body is one and has many members, and all the members of the body, though many, are one body, so it is with Christ. For by one Spirit we were all baptised into one body – Jews or Greeks, slaves or free – and all were made to drink of the one Spirit.'

---

* At the time this sermon was preached, the Liturgical Commission had recently published the *Alternative Services Book*. This was a temporary revision to be later replaced in 2000 by a number of service books, published under the general title *Common Worship*.

PREACHING TO THE CROWD

(A sermon on the text Luke 5: 1–11, preached at the Eucharist in St Alban's Church, Wood Street, Guildford on Septuagesima Sunday 2004.)

Let us picture the scene. Jesus was standing by the lakeside. There was a vast crowd of people. They had been following him for some days, bringing their sick to be cured, hoping for more miracles. Not only that: they wanted to hear him preach, for he was not only a healer. He was a powerful speaker with a reputation which had spread through the region.

As the crowd pressed upon Jesus, he caught sight of Simon Peter in a boat. He called him over, got in and asked him to row a short distance away from the shore. Seeing him being rowed away the crowd must have thought he was leaving them. But then he stopped the boat, stood up and began to preach, and they realised why he had got into the boat. Sound carries further across water. The crowd could now hear his voice more clearly than if he had stood in their midst.

We are not told how many people there were. We have to guess. But we know that on another occasion the crowd numbered five thousand. There is no reason why a similar or even greater number of people were not gathered at the lakeside on this occasion. But would they have been able to hear? Would Jesus's voice, unaided by the modern technology of amplification, have carried?

We forget how audible, how effective, the natural voice can be when it is correctly projected.

John Wesley and the pioneer preachers of Methodism 250 years ago would speak to huge open-air audiences, numbering thousands. In the eighteenth century, Benjamin Franklin in

America carried out an experiment. He wanted to test the truth of reports that George Whitefield (the famous preacher) could be heard by huge outdoor audiences. He went to hear him preach in the open in Philadelphia. Franklin began by standing close to the preacher. He then moved away, pushing himself towards the back. He carried on until he could no longer hear the preacher's words. There he stopped. Then, after the sermon was over and the crowd had dispersed, he paced the distance between where he was at the limit of audibility to the platform on which Whitehead had been standing. He then calculated the area of ground in a semicircle of radius equal to that distance. Then he divided that area by the space each standing person would occupy (he reckoned two square feet). The answer he came to was 30,000.

Given the right conditions – a still evening, a favourable slope, a good speaker, or in the case of today's story, a stretch of flat water – it is possible for the unaided human voice to be heard by 30,000 people.

Jesus knew the importance of the big audience. He used it to great effect, but he backed up his ministry to the crowd with careful instruction of the few. He built his church upon the tiny handful of disciples, not upon a strategy of mass conversion. Today's story shows him moving away from the crowd after he had finished his sermon, and concentrating upon the small group of Peter, James and John.

In our own generation many have turned to Christ as a result of being moved by the words of a great preacher or attending a student Christian rally, or a Christian summer camp, or worshipping amongst the huge congregations at Taizé, or a pilgrimage to Lourdes.

In these ways the Spirit of the Lord speaks through the great event with its highly charged atmosphere and its almost tangible sense of wonder and devotion. Many of you will have known such an experience – when a flame was kindled in your heart and God seemed very close. For some of us it happened years ago – for some it might have happened last summer – for some it has yet to happen.

But whatever our different experience of conversion may be – of conversion, that is, by means of the big event – we are all drawn by God through a quite different process of conversion; conversion by means of little events.

After we have heard the voice speaking across the lake, after the excitement of the crowd, he takes us aside to join a small, rather uncertain group of disciples. He then sets to work on the lifelong process of our conversion. Three steps forward. Two steps back. Sometimes two steps forward and three steps back. Sometimes no visible progress at all, just a period of marking time. But little by little, if we allow, he draws us onwards and closer to himself.

The process of conversion is never complete. There is always another step ahead. St Richard of Chichester knew this when he wrote in his famous prayer:

Thanks be to thee, my Lord Jesus Christ,
For all the benefits thou hast given me,
For all the pains and insults thou hast borne for me.
Most merciful Redeemer, Friend and Brother,
May I know thee more clearly,
Love thee more dearly,
And follow thee more nearly,
Day by day. Amen.

SURVIVOR OF *LA BELLE EPOQUE*

Ninian Comper
1864–1960
Church Architect and Designer

(First published in the *Church Times*, December 2012.)

Ninian Comper's church architecture, woodwork and silver, textile designs and stained glass brought colour and elegance to many churches and cathedrals in the first half of the twentieth century. His earlier work was strongly influenced by the late perpendicular style of the fifteenth century; he was regarded as the last of the Gothic Revivalists. Later, he created an eclectic style of his own in which he mixed classical with medieval and renaissance forms. He was knighted in 1950.

Comper had his critics. Pevsner claimed that although the rood screen, organ case and pulpit in St Mary's, Egmanton, Nottinghamshire (1897) were admirable as pastiche, 'as pieces of contemporary art they are all of course valueless'. The 'of course' betrays an arrogance unworthy of its author.

Comper also had his admirers. Peter Anson in his authoritative *Fashions in Church Furnishing 1840–1940* described Comper's early work at St Cyprian's, Clarence Gate (1902), with its white interior, graceful columns, delicate screen and gorgeous textiles, as being redolent of Edwardian luxury, putting him in mind of *pêche Melba*. Comper, more soberly, described it as a setting fit for the liturgy of the Book of Common Prayer. And much more than a mere setting: 'A church is its own prayer,' he wrote, 'and should bring you to your knees when you enter.'

Later, he created an inclusive style influenced by his study of the fusion of classical Greek, Saracenic and Gothic styles in Sicily and elsewhere, and of the English seventeenth-century combination of classical with Gothic. All styles, he wrote, even those of pagan antiquity, could contribute to 'unity by inclusion'. In St Mary's, Wellingborough (1904–1931) he designed Gothic arches to rest upon fluted Greek columns headed by Corinthians capitals, and a classical *baldachino* to surmount a free-standing altar. One may make a 'virtual tour' online of his work (google 'Ninian Comper' and then 'images').

Betjeman wrote of Comper's church designs, 'I saw... proportion, attention to detail, colour, texture and chiefly purpose – the tabernacle as the centre of it all.' It was Comper's aim to draw attention to the altar, at first with his design of the Gothic altar with riddel posts hung with richly embroidered curtains and surmounted by gilded angels, and later by the introduction of a free-standing altar beneath a baldachin, a majestic canopy in wood or stone supported by columns (e.g. St Philip's Cosham, 1937).

In his 1912 re-ordering of the Grosvenor Chapel, South Audley Street, he brought the altar forward, placed it under a baldachin west of the screened chancel, thereby creating the Lady Chapel east of the screen.

His chancel screens, surmounted by the rood with accompanying figures, were designed with exuberant élan. Whether in a large building like St Mary's, Egmanton or a tiny Cornish church like St Petroc's, Little Petherick, these magnificent structures with their open tracery, painted saints and gilded seraphim, far from obscuring the sanctuary, serve as a portal, drawing the eye along a lengthened vista to the dazzling altar beyond.

His painted glass is characterised by its lightness, the rich blues and reds enhanced by areas of clear glass, giving a translucent effect. His depiction of *Christos Pantokrator*, showing a youthful unbearded figure seated in majesty, recurs in a number of east windows (Downside Abbey, Pusey House, Southwark Cathedral are three). In these you catch the serene glory which shines through all his work.

Many of his commissions were from private patrons. Athelstan Riley (St Petroc), Lord Shaftesbury (Wimbourne), the Nugée family (Cosham), Edward Brook (Ufford), the Childers family (Cantley), Lord Halifax (Hickley), the Duke of Newcastle (Egmanton) are a few of many. Had he been born a century later, it is unlikely that his work would have prospered without the benefit of such notable patronage.

Comper was described as a 'mysterious figure', hard to categorise. 'An aesthete who dressed with understated elegance,' according to his biographer Fr Anthony Symondson SJ. He spoke 'in an exquisitely modulated voice'; a raconteur of the *fin de siècle* who had known Aubrey Beardsley and his circle, and who had lived through the Second World War and its *après la guerre* barbarism. Betjeman recalled how Comper had winced at the corduroy breeches of the two beefy land-girls to whom they had given a lift near Marlborough: 'Oh that uniform!' groaned the survivor of *La Belle Epoque*. 'It shows a lack of reverence to Our Lady.'

But for Comper love of beauty was much more than the affectation of an aesthete; it was a doorway into the presence of God. His life's work was to create church interiors which would evoke from the casual visitor and the regular worshipper alike the response, 'This is none other than the house of God; this is the gate of heaven.'

THE HABERDASHER OF EAST GRINSTEAD

John Mason Neale
1818–1866
Priest, Hymn-Writer and Founder of the
Society of St Margaret, East Grinstead

(First published in the *Church Times*, August 2009.)

John Mason Neale's nurse described him as the dearest and dirtiest boy she had ever known. Her affectionate exasperation was shared by friends and colleagues throughout his turbulent, brilliant and brief career. He died aged only forty-eight, having worn himself out as priest, pastor and writer.

He was an Anglican priest, and a leading nineteenth-century liturgical scholar, hymn-writer and church historian. He was a founder member of the Cambridge Camden Society (later called the Ecclesiological Society) whose aim was to apply Tractarian principles to church architecture, furnishing and liturgy. For almost all of his working life he was Warden of Sackville College, a foundation for poor pensioners at East Grinstead. He founded the Society of St Margaret, a teaching and nursing sisterhood.

His enthusiasm for the restoration of order and beauty in Anglican worship brought him into conflict with his bishop, Dr Gilbert. On visiting the chapel of Sackville College, recently refurbished by Neale, and seeing there a cross, a pair of candlesticks and an embroidered cloth upon the altar, Gilbert flew into a rage and placed Neale under a ban for 'debasing the minds of these poor people with his spiritual haberdashery'. He could not sack him, as the college was outside episcopal jurisdiction, but he could withhold his licence to officiate as a priest. The inhibition was upheld by the Court of Arches, and for some years Neale was obliged to conduct prayers as a layman in the dining room, being careful not to wear a surplice and not to utter the priestly words of absolution in public worship.

It was a grievous position for a conscientious pastor to be placed in. Some, including Bishop Wilberforce of Oxford and Earl De La Warr, patron of the college, thought it was ludicrous and said so. But there were many clergy who agreed with Bishop Gilbert, and in those days it was an easy matter to stir up a hostile mob. When the Vicar of East Grinstead put it about that the Warden of Sackville College was 'a papistical mountebank' – his offence on that occasion having been to cover the coffin at the funeral of one his pensioners with a cross-embroidered pall – the people rioted, seized the coffin and set fire to the college.

Some years later another riot broke out in Lewes at the funeral of one of the sisters of the Society of St Margaret. Dark rumours were spread concerning the causes of the sister's death (she had, in fact, died from scarlet fever caught from a patient). Her father, the vicar of a parish in Lewes, published a pamphlet denouncing Neale as a 'Puseyite Jesuit'. The people of Lewes, goaded beyond reason by such language, tried to lynch Neale.

It is remarkable that he and his family survived such violent and malicious hostility. They rose above the storms. There is evidence from family papers that they enjoyed much happiness in their home at Sackville College. Despite his unremitting work – he rose at 4.30am and wrote into the night – Neale was an attentive and loving husband and father. There were visits to the travelling circus, picnics on festival days, concerts at Exeter Hall and the Crystal Palace, indoor games at home and, according to the children, not once were they told, 'Hush, Papa is working,' even though the nursery was directly above his study. He did not complain of interruption, though it was quite normal for him to have sixteen different literary projects on hand at any one time, ranging from his commentary on the psalms, his history of the Eastern Church, articles for the Ecclesiologist ('Twenty-Three Reasons for Getting Rid of Church Pews') to writing hymns ('Good King Wenceslas'), translating Latin ones ('Jerusalem the Golden'), compiling editions of ancient Syriac texts, and writing children's stories.

On Sundays and feast days, the twenty or so pensioners were invited to dine with the family. The toast was always given by old Mrs Elizabeth Alcock. 'Well, sir, here's your good health and all your family's,' she would say, continuing:

Long may you live,
Happy may you be,
From misfortune free,
And blest with eternitee.

He found contentment in the collegiate life. Occasionally, trouble arose. An outbreak of petty vandalism was traced to one of the inmates. A private detective, Mr Field, was hired, and for days he haunted the cloisters disguised as a French polisher. Charges were brought, but the suspect was acquitted. She then brought charges against the Warden (she was put up to this by the *Brighton Gazette*). The matter was resolved when she died.

In 1854 Neale founded the Community of St Margaret, a teaching and nursing order of nuns. The sisters taught in an orphanage and a school, as well as nursing in some of the poorest cottages in the region. Neale was their spiritual guide and chaplain. Katherine Egerton, who became Mother Superior, recalled in her memoir, 'Those marvellous sermons [in the oratory] on the Religious Life... as if the gates of heaven were opened and revealed the company therein.'

THE SACKVILLE VAULT

'I don't suppose anyone has been down here since my father-in-law died,' said the Countess as she unlocked the door to the vault, 'and that was over twenty years ago.'

I was expecting all sorts of horrors as we descended a flight of stone steps into the Sackville vault. It was a surprise then to find the air fresh and dry, without a hint of mustiness or damp. We were standing in a well-ventilated chamber, about twelve by eighteen feet. The vault was lined with large stone shelves set into arched niches in the north and south walls. On these shelves rested the coffins of former Sackvilles, dating back to the reign of Elizabeth I. The purpose of our visit was to inspect the vault before the reception later that week of the coffin of the late Dowager Countess.

'That's the tenth Earl,' the Countess said, pointing to a coffin which lay on a heavily built table in the centre of the chamber. 'We always leave the last one there, until the next arrival. Then he or she joins the others on the shelves.'

In the light of our torches we could see around us generations of Sackvilles, the most recent members identifiable by the inscriptions on their silver coffin-plates. One of the coffins retained its velvet covering, a funerary coronet still in place upon the top.

The wooden coffins of earlier Sackvilles had long ago fallen into dust, leaving only the inner casing of lead enclosing the mortal remains. At the back of the shelves our torches could barely make out the crumpled sheets of lead, impacted upon each other under their own weight and no longer recognisable as individual caskets.

This remarkable family had been present at many of the great moments of English history. The first Lord Buckhurst had carried the news from Westminster to Mary Queen of Scots at Fotheringhay Castle that Parliament had passed a bill for her execution. The sixth Earl, a poet and rake, had offered his mistress, Nell Gwyn, to Charles II. The seventh Earl had travelled to Hanover in 1714 to summon the Elector George to be our king. He was later elevated to a dukedom. The third Duke played cricket for Kent and, whilst serving as our ambassador to France, invited a team to Paris. Unhappily the Revolution intervened and the cricketers got no further than Dover. Otherwise, how different might have been the history of that troubled country had her nobility resided on their estates and learnt to engage with their tenants on the cricket field as had ours in England. The ninth Earl De La Warr (the dukedom had become extinct in 1845) was the first peer to serve in a Labour government.

'Man is a noble animal, splendid in ashes, and pompous in the grave, solemnising nativities and deaths with equal lustre, nor omitting ceremonies of bravery, in the infamy of his nature.' So wrote the seventeenth-century Norwich physician Sir Thomas Browne in his *Urn Burial*. He understood that we solemnise the sacred mystery of death with ceremonies and funerary pomp, not for our vainglory, but in recognition of the transience of human achievement; to point up the contrast between our trophies and the 'infamy of our nature'.

As we were about to climb the steps out of the vault, I noticed a wooden box, too small and the wrong shape to be a coffin for human remains.

'What's that?' I asked.

'One of the dogs. William insisted.'

As we re-entered the church we passed through the Sackville chapel, situated above the vault. It is lit by a large east window depicting in stained glass the heraldic family history.

At its foot there is the legend in Latin: *Nobilis familia Sackville hic expectat Resurrectionem.*

Here the noble family of Sackville awaits the Resurrection.

MAIMONIDES AND THE CAIRO GENIZA

(From an article first published in the *Church Times*, 19 November 2004.)

In 1864 Jacob Saphir, a Talmudic scholar from Lithuania, visited the crumbling Ben Ezra synagogue in Fustat (Old Cairo). He had heard stories about a hidden chamber, stacked to its roof with thousands of ancient documents, the written records of a once-thriving Jewish community. What he found – though it took scholars some decades to recognise their importance – was a vast jumble of letters, petitions, title deeds, wills, court depositions, inventories, business accounts, religious rulings and contracts, written in Hebrew, Arabic, Coptic, Latin, Syriac, Aramaic, Castilian, Georgian and Ladino, an ancient Jewish dialect from Spain.

What emerged from this pile of dusty fragments – discarded, but not destroyed lest they contain the sacred Name – was a portrait of a community which had lived and traded in what was during the eleventh and twelfth centuries one of the world's largest and busiest cities.

The voices of husbands and wives, fathers and sons, creditors and debtors, plaintiffs and defendants, buyers and sellers – the whole hubbub of city life came tumbling out of that great archive known to scholars as the Cairo *Geniza*. It is the noise of a Jewish community not set apart in a ghetto, but deeply enmeshed in a cosmopolitan and pluralist society. Shared ownership of properties crossed confessional boundaries. Business partnerships between Jew, Christian and Muslim were commonplace. Documents record that such partnerships were confirmed before Muslim and rabbinic courts. In one fragment we read of a Christian asking a Muslim court to ratify the sale of his share of the property to his Jewish business partner.

As leader of the Jewish community, the great scholar Maimonides (*Moses ben Maimon* or, in Arabic, *Abū ʿImran Mūsā ibn Maymūn*) was frequently called upon to make judgements upon situations arising from life in the cosmopolitan city. In one such case, the Jewish and Muslim owners of a glass-making workshop, which employed workers of both religions, had sought his ruling upon their decision that the workshop could stay open seven days a week, so long as the gains made upon Friday were paid exclusively to the Jewish workers, and those on Saturday to the Muslims. Was this arrangement in accordance with Jewish law? Maimonides agreed that it was.

The *Geniza* documents give us glimpses of social and religious life in twelfth-century Cairo. The city's calendar was influenced partly by the arrivals and departures of the great trade caravans, and partly by the religious festivals of the different communities. It was not unusual for people to participate in the non-liturgical aspects of each other's religious celebrations. Members of the Caliph's court, as well as the general population, would join the street celebrations at the Christian feast of the Epiphany. Members of all three religions would join the annual procession to Giza to visit the prison in which Potiphar had imprisoned the Patriarch Joseph. Each Friday the Muslim population would attend prayers at the great Mosque of Amr at the heart of the commercial centre in Fustat, and the non-Muslim citizens would wait to witness the arrival of the Caliph on those occasions when he chose to lead the prayers.

Proximity at home and at work between Jew, Christian and Muslim, as well as familiarity with the religious observances of each other's faiths, inevitably created in the minds of the citizens a relaxed attitude to the exclusive claims of their own and their neighbours' beliefs. It was an attitude which, in the case of the better-educated, dared to measure the claims of sacred revelation made in the Hebrew Torah, the Christian Gospel or the Muslim Koran, against the claims of rational philosophy, the natural sciences and, as is ever the case, the exigencies of daily life.

THE ARCHBISHOP WHO CROSSED FRONTIERS

William Temple 1881–1944
Archbishop of Canterbury

(First published in the *Church Times*, November 2008.)

'To a man of my generation,' wrote George Bernard Shaw, 'an archbishop of Temple's enlightenment was a realised impossibility.' It was William Temple's ability to speak across the frontiers of church and state, of belief and unbelief, which made so many listen. When he died in 1944 at the early age of sixty-three, people believed that not only the church but the country had lost a leader.

He had been born into the purple – his father had been Archbishop of Canterbury – but as a young man he was ready, if necessary, to stand outside the church establishment. In matters of belief he approached the articles of faith with an open mind. It was his 'tentative assent' (his words) to belief in the Virgin Birth and the Bodily Resurrection of Our Lord that delayed his ordination. 'Tentative' was not good enough. The Bishop of Oxford firmly, but courteously, asked for greater conviction. In time Temple came to that conviction, but his journey to that position made him all the more accessible to those who did not or could not follow him.

He was for that reason an effective apologist for Christian belief. His broadcasts, his speeches and his articles reached a vast audience. He was able to communicate particularly well with students, his mission addresses to the universities being always packed with both believers and unbelievers. He did much to support the work of the Student Christian Movement.

He was able to engage at an individual level with non-believers. 'I remember,' he wrote, 'once saying to Bertie Russell: "I believe in [the Resurrection] far more than the evidence warrants." Bertie said: "And I *disbelieve* it far more."' It was an interesting admission by the nation's leading atheist to the nation's leading Christian that he, too, based his belief (or disbelief) on an act of faith.

As a young man he had been vigorously critical of the church's apparent reluctance to face the moral and social issues of education, housing and poverty. He had had first-hand experience of impoverishment of large sections of the population from his visits as an undergraduate to the university settlements in Bethnal Green and Bermondsey. 'Inasmuch as ye did it not unto the least of these…' he would often quote.

From 1908 to 1924 he was president of the Workers' Education Association and was indefatigable in promoting its work in speeches up and down the country and articles in the national press. During the First World War his name was on the police list of dangerous persons because of his prominence in the WEA. Later, he did not let the growing burden of episcopal duties diminish his advocacy for the oppressed. His book *Christianity and Social Order* (1942) rapidly sold 139,000 copies. In 1938 he chaired a committee investigating unemployment, and published *Men Without Work.*

He described himself as a Broad Churchman and was impatient with narrow distinctions of churchmanship. He took a lead in the ecumenical movement and was an effective supporter of the formation of the Church of South India, as well of the establishment of the British Council of Churches in 1942.

A brief notice like this of Temple's colossal output of work as bishop, teacher, writer and broadcaster, runs the risk of becoming an incomplete catalogue, quite missing the humanity and the fun of the man. His mirth was famous and infectious – on one occasion he was asked to moderate his laughter or leave the theatre. He was formidable on the tennis court, less so on the links. After a stiff climb in the Lake District he loved to tuck into a huge farmhouse tea of bread, butter, cream and bilberry jam. On hearing of Temple's death, a Cumbrian dales-man said, 'He was a very *jolly* man.'

Above all, what won so many hearts was his humanity, which was 'founded on his love of God and fortified by massive knowledge, absolute simplicity, and a sincerity that was beyond question' (FA Iremonger, *William Temple*, 1948).

THE CLERIC WHO DISCOVERED PREHISTORY

William Buckland
1784–1856
Geologist, Clergyman and Eccentric

(First published in the *Church Times*, 9 August 2013.)

Buckland, with his bag full of fossils, changed everything. In the crowded lecture room at the Old Ashmolean in Oxford, where he enlivened his lectures with imitations of the gait of extinct reptiles; in the senior common rooms over port and snuff; on horseback in the field where he took his students on site visits; at the dinner table of country houses where he was a convivial guest; in his canon's lodgings at Christ Church where he and his wife were generous hosts; this amiable and loquacious clergyman changed the mental landscape of nineteenth-century England.

The Reverend William Buckland would ride up and down the country on his favourite black mare, exploring caves and rocks, before returning to the lecture room at Oxford with bits of stone, the skull of a hyena, the teeth of a mammoth and the fossilised faeces of a prehistoric reptile. The audience at his popular lectures during the 1820's included Thomas Arnold, Samuel Wilberforce, Newman, Pusey, Keble and Charles Lyell, who became Darwin's geological mentor. Theirs was the first generation to be confronted with the evidence of a prehistoric Britain, where tigers and hippos roamed the land. The conclusions they drew were varied and contradictory, but one thing was sure: they could never again read the early chapters of the Book of Genesis in quite the same simplistic way as had their fathers.

Buckland had a well-developed sense of taste. On being asked about the small stains which kept reappearing on a cathedral floor, he knelt down, licked the marks and identified their source as bat urine. He knew the flavour. The story was told that over port after dinner at Nuneham Courtney, when his host passed round the table a highly prized possession – the mummified heart of Louis XIV, now shrunk to the size and appearance of pickled walnut – the elderly Buckland absent-mindedly popped it into his mouth and swallowed it.

He once claimed that it was his intention 'to eat his way through the animal kingdom', an ambition which was partly realised by the exotic range of dishes put before his guests at Christ Church, dishes which included ostrich, crocodile steak and hedgehog. It had been one of the purposes of the London Zoological Society, of which he was a founder member, to extend the human diet in a world of growing population and diminishing resources.

His hospitality at Christ Church was well known. Ruskin always regretted that because of a previous engagement he had missed the opportunity to eat toasted mouse. A young Florence Nightingale recorded her delight when, during her visit to Canon Buckland, they were accompanied at table by a young bear, which then had to be sent out of the room in disgrace for grabbing the butter.

Behind the buffoonery and pranks (Darwin was *not* amused) there was a serious and brilliant mind. His two-volume contribution to the Bridgewater Treatises (1836), which was five years in preparation, left no one in any doubt of that. It was because Buckland despaired of the university's ever according his subject a proper place in the curriculum that he left academia to become Dean of Westminster. 'Some years ago,' he wrote in 1847, 'I was sanguine as to the possibility of Natural History making progress in Oxford, but I have long come to the conclusion that it is utterly hopeless.'

At Westminster he was indefatigable, especially in his efforts to modernise the school drains. According to the memoir written by his son, F T Buckland, 'Rising soon after seven, he worked incessantly till two and three o'clock the next morning.' At Islip (he held the living *in commendam* with the deanery) he laid out allotments for the labourers and built a recreation room for the parish youth.

His declining years were clouded by mental illness, thought to have been caused by an injury sustained when the carriage in which he was travelling overturned and threw him and Mrs Buckland heavily to the ground. He died in an asylum in Clapham on 14 August 1856.

CAN THESE BONES LIVE?

We took the road from Cairo towards Wadi Natrun, a desolate depression in Egypt's western desert. It derives its name from the ancient word for the saline deposit used in the process of mummifying the dead and had been extensively mined there during the times of the pharaohs. Later, during Egypt's Christian pre-Islamic period, the presence of water and the remoteness of the region attracted large numbers of hermits and monks to its bleak landscape.

We made our visit in January 1953. Ahead of us stood one of the four surviving monasteries, marooned in a vast sea of sand and enclosed by high walls. Fifteen centuries earlier, in the late fourth century, the historian Rufinus of Aquileia had made the same journey. He recorded his arrival thus:

> *As we were drawing near the place, as soon as the monks knew that strange brethren were coming, straightway they poured out like a swarm of bees, each from his cell and ran to meet us, joyous and eager, the most part carrying pitchers of water and bread.*

In 1953 things were different. The community was on the verge of collapse. Few pilgrims came to visit. Tourists were rare. Sheltered within those broken buildings we found a handful of ageing monks, the tattered remnant of a community that went back sixteen centuries to their founder, St Macarius. Inside, we were shown the ruinous chapel where the brothers gathered daily for prayers and celebrated the ancient Coptic liturgy every Sunday.

At the age of fourteen I was too young to grasp fully the meaning of this extraordinary place. To me it breathed desolation. The crumbling masonry, the drifts of dirt and sand in the passageways, the broken lattice screens in the chapel, the ragged vestments and stained hangings, the torn texts slipping from a lop-sided lectern and the partially defaced paintings on the walls told a story of utter hopelessness and neglect. In a corner lay the shrivelled corpse of a small creature, probably a rat, its desiccated skin lying loose upon its bones.

We saw an ostrich egg hanging from the chancel vault, its silver chain black with neglect. The guide told us that it was there to remind the monks that God was watching over them with his protective gaze. It was an ancient belief that the ostrich incubated its eggs by gazing at them. According to legend it would dig a shallow depression in the sand in which to lay its eggs and then retreat some yards before settling down to watch, the force of its gaze generating new life within the shells. It was a symbol of divine protection and generation.

We were shown into the refectory, a dark, low, foul-smelling chamber. A few small loaves of 'flat bread', some dates and dried beans had been placed on the stone ledge that served as a table, and now awaited the monks' collection. Their rule, in those times, did not permit the conviviality of a shared meal except on Sunday.

Outside, sitting in the shade against a wall was a blind beggar, one of those strays who find refuge in religious communities. As he turned his face up at me I saw that his eyes were clouded by a thick, white film, a common affliction those days amongst the Egyptian *fellahin*. 'Bakshheesh,' he mumbled, holding out his hand for money. We caught glimpses of other figures as they scuttled off into the shadows of the narrow passages which intersected the tumbled buildings.

I cannot pretend that I gave that visit much thought in the years that followed. When I considered it at all, I pictured those ruins as they might now be, covered by an advancing tide of sand as the desert reclaimed her old domain.

I was quite wrong.

Recently I happened to be searching the web for some information – I cannot recall what – when there came up on the screen, unbidden, words I had not heard spoken or seen written in nearly seventy years: *Wadi Natrun.* The story they told is a remarkable one.*

In 1969 the Coptic Pope, Cyril VI, initiated a period of restoration. He ordered twelve selected monks from elsewhere in Egypt to join the six remaining monks at the monastery of St Macarius (*Abu Maqar*). Their mission was to revive the spiritual life of the community and to restore the buildings. To prepare themselves for their task they spent ten years in solitude and prayer before moving to Wadi Natrun.

By the close of the twentieth century the monastery had been rebuilt and enlarged, covering an area six times greater than before. The community had grown to more than a hundred. By their labour the monks had reclaimed and brought under cultivation large areas of the surrounding desert; a printing press had been set up; youth training programmes established; a road built for the bus-loads of tourists and the steady stream of pilgrims who come regularly to marvel at the ancient murals, now restored, to pray, to attend retreats and to find spiritual refreshment in the desert.

'Son of man, can these bones live?' God asked the prophet Ezekiel at the valley of dry bones. 'O Lord God, you know,' Ezekiel replied as his gaze took in that ghastly sight. 'Prophesy,' he was told, 'Prophesy to these bones, and say to them, O dry bones, hear the word of the Lord.'

As the Spirit of God moved across the scene a gaze more searching than Ezekiel's stirred new life in the wilderness.

---

* www.stmacariusmonastery.org

A HANOVERIAN PRELATE

Thomas Secker
1693–1768
Archbishop of Canterbury

(First published in the *Church Times*, August 2012.)

Speak, look and move with dignity and ease;
Like mitred Secker, you'll be sure to please.

This was the advice given to aspiring clergy. Thomas Secker's *curriculum vitae* seems to confirm a later generation's opinion of eighteenth-century bishops: worldly, pluralist, time-serving. Closer examination of his life reveals a careful pastor, an industrious administrator and a conscientious priest.

Thomas Secker was educated at Samuel Jones's dissenters' academy in Tewkesbury. He took Anglican orders after a brief sojourn at Oxford University. Winning favour with Queen Caroline, he gained rapid preferment, becoming in turn Rector of Houghton le Spring, Canon of Durham, Chaplain to the Royal Household, Rector of St James's, Piccadilly, Bishop of Bristol, Bishop of Oxford, Dean of St Paul's and finally in 1758 Archbishop of Canterbury.

As Rector of St James's, Piccadilly and at the same time Bishop of Oxford, Secker balanced the demands of his busy London parish with those of his diocese by spending autumn, winter and spring at his London rectory, and summer at his episcopal palace near Oxford. At St James's he preached in the morning on three Sundays in the month and on the fourth at one of the two chapels which were then in the parish. He catechised every Sunday evening, and on weekdays during Lent he gave a course of lectures. As bishop he held annual confirmations at St James's, having examined the candidates himself after giving them a course of instruction over the preceding four to six weeks. He contributed regularly to the debates in the House of Lords and took turn as duty chaplain to the royal household.

On the Wednesday in Whit week every year he departed for Cuddesdon Palace, his episcopal residence near Oxford. There he would remain for three or four months to discharge his duties of diocesan visitation and confirmation, as well as correspondence and interviews with his clergy. His letters to his clergy reveal a vigilant diocesan, exacting high standards of his priests and correcting back-sliders. He encouraged more frequent Holy Communion and effective preaching. 'We have lost many people to the sectaries by not preaching in a manner sufficiently evangelical.' He held ordinations three times a year at Christ Church Cathedral. During the remaining months he left the diocese to the charge of his archdeacons.

After sixteen years, he admitted he was tired. He was offered the Deanery of St Paul's as a rest cure. The post was described by Archbishop Herring as offering *otium cum dignitate* (leisure with dignity). On accepting the deanery Secker resigned his Durham prebend and the Rectory of St James but retained his Bishopric of Oxford. During his eight years at St Paul's he put the finances on to a sound footing, organised the cathedral records (indexing them in his own hand), corrected the statutes and established a programme of building repair.

In March 1758 he became Archbishop of Canterbury. Lambeth Palace was in a ruinous state and in need of repair having been unoccupied for years. In July he conducted his primary diocesan visitation, issuing articles of enquiry to the clergy, delivering his charge and holding fifteen services of confirmation during that year. The diocese had known nothing like it. In his charges and his sermons, he stressed the centrality of Christ's atoning sacrifice on the Cross, to the discomfort of his latitudinarian critics who accused him of papistry.

He was buried, according to his instructions, beneath the passage between Lambeth Palace and the adjacent church. On a black marble slab were inscribed, without adornment or epitaph, the words:

Thomas Secker, Archbishop of Canterbury,
died 3 August 1768, aged seventy-five.

PIONEER OF SOCIAL HOUSING

Octavia Hill
1838–1912
Social Reformer and Co-Founder of the National Trust

(First published in the *Church Times*, August 2010.)

Octavia Hill was described by some as a kindly soul, but those who worked with her saw a more steely side. Henrietta Barnet spoke of ruthlessness. Gertrude Bell called her despotic. The Bishop of London, Frederick Temple, had a bruising encounter with her at a meeting of the Ecclesiastical Commissioners. 'She spoke for half an hour... I never had such a beating in all my life.'

She was the ninth child of a wealthy East Anglian corn merchant, whose bankruptcy and mental breakdown cast a deep shadow over her childhood. Educated at home by her mother and imbued from an early age by the progressive principles of her grandfather, Southwood Smith, the health reformer and social campaigner, she devoted her life to the urban poor, and in particular to housing reform.

Charles Kingsley and F D Maurice gave a Christian focus to her socialism. She was fourteen when she and her sister began to attend daily Morning Prayer at Lincoln's Inn, where Maurice was chaplain. Until then there had been no formal religion in her upbringing. 'It was Mr Maurice who showed me a life in the Creeds, the services and the Bible; who interpreted for me much that was dark and puzzling in life.' He prepared her for baptism and confirmation.

Ruskin met her at the Ladies Co-operative Guild in Russell Place where her mother was manager. The Guild provided training and employment for the poor. At thirteen 'Ocky' studied glass painting in the Guild workshop. A year later she was in charge of the toy-making shop where she instructed children from the ragged school. Later, Ruskin employed her in copying works of art to illustrate his *Modern Painters*.

Octavia had a commanding presence. At the age of thirteen, alone in the house one Sunday, she surprised a burglar emerging from a cupboard upstairs. 'How did you come up here?' she asked. 'I came up the stairs,' he said. 'Then you will please to walk down again.' And he did, down two flights and out into the street with her close behind.

Despite her assertiveness, her letters reveal how submissive she was to her mentor. For ten years Ruskin made use of her skill at copying. She persuaded herself that this drudgery was a necessary development of her art. It was, ironically, Ruskin himself who provided an escape. On his father's death he was able out of his inheritance to pay for Octavia's first housing scheme.

Ruskin put up the money to buy three adjacent houses and repair them. She instituted a regime of regular rent collection. To help tenants she set up saving schemes and employed defaulters on maintenance work on their own and other dwellings. She, and later the housing managers whom she trained, made a weekly round to collect the rent and listen to the tenants. The scheme was small-scale, direct, personal. It was a beginning.

She insisted on paying Ruskin a five per cent return on his investment. Not only the tenants, but the scheme too must pay its way. Later, when she had become a member of the Royal Commission for the Poor Law, she remained deeply opposed to state or municipal provision of housing and welfare, to the dismay of her fellow members Beatrice Webb and George Lansbury. She said, 'We have made many mistakes with our alms: eaten out the heart of the independent, bolstered up the drunkard... discouraged thrift.'

The Ecclesiastical Commissioners asked her to manage much of their property in Southwark, Walworth and Deptford. She insisted that the rebuilt housing should be predominantly two-storey cottages with public space for gardens, and that blocks of flats should not be higher than three storeys. Over twenty years the commissioners transferred more and more properties as the former leases fell in. In 1903, for example, she oversaw and managed the redevelopment of one large South London estate, housing 700 families in newly built four- and six-roomed cottages.

She believed that people in town, especially the poor, must have access to green space. She encouraged the tenants of the Redcross cottages in Southwark to hold a flower show. Concerts were held in the hall. The cottages and hall still stand. She campaigned for the protection of London's parks and gardens – what she called the people's 'open air sitting rooms'. She was a founder member of the National Trust and a champion of public rights of way.

In old age she could be met clearing the footpaths near her country retreat, swishing her stick at the nettles and cow parsley with the same vigour which she had once used to face down a bishop and expel a burglar.

A GP'S TAKE ON RELIGION

Sir Thomas Browne
1605–1682
Physician and Author

(First published in the *Church Times*, 18 October 2012.)

Thomas Browne was born in London on 19 October 1605. He was educated at Winchester and Oxford, and studied medicine on the continent. He was a general practitioner in Norwich for nearly fifty years. His written works include *Urn Burial*, *The Garden of Cyrus* and *Religio Medici*. He was happily married and the father of a large family. He died on his seventy-seventh birthday, 19 October 1682, and was buried in the chancel of St Peter Mancroft, Norwich.

For my religion, though there be several circumstances that might persuade the world I have none at all, as the general scandal of my profession, the natural course of my studies, the indifferency of my behaviour and discourse in matters of religion, neither violently defending one, nor with that common ardour and contention opposing another; yet in despite hereof, I dare, without usurpation, assume the honourable style of Christian.

Religio Medici

He might have put it more briefly, and simply told us that he was a doctor who believed in God. But the glory of Thomas Browne's prose is that it was never simple and rarely brief. The modern ear, fearful of the dependant clause, might be baffled by this opening sentence of *Religio Medici*. It needs, however, only a measure of perseverance before we pick up the rhythm and are drawn into the mind of this engaging and sagacious physician.

He takes us by the hand into his library for a leisurely exposition of his religious beliefs. His tone is confidential, almost deferential. We feel that he is a reticent man, and yet he desires our company, perhaps our approval. We are surprised that one so young (he is only thirty) should have settled opinions upon such a wide variety of topics.

We are, perhaps, intimidated by his great learning, lightly worn. However, we are flattered by his assumption that we can recognise, without recourse to footnotes, the allusions which illuminate his text. And it is not only examples from classical antiquity which tumble from his pen, but also references to contemporary scientific research being conducted in the medical schools of Montpellier, Padua and Leyden.

What delights the reader is Browne's wry 'take' on life. The 'scandal of his profession', as he calls it, allows him to view the human condition from the oblique perspective of a GP. He had good precedent. St Luke, also a physician, lightened his narrative in the *Acts* with similar irony.

Rare among his contemporaries, Browne was able to bring a healing touch to the rancour of theological debate. At a time when feelings about the conduct of worship ran so high that men came to blows over whether or not to kneel at prayer, he was able to write: 'I am, I confess, naturally inclined to that which misguided zeal terms superstition. At my devotion I love to use the civility of my knee, my hat, and hand.'

When the matter is put like that, who could quarrel with the sign of the cross? Who could cavil at a genuflexion?

As a layman he was able to put the case for the *via media* of the Church of England with a clarity equal to Hooker's. 'In brief where scripture is silent, the church is my text; where that speaks, 'tis but my comment: where there is a joint silence of both, I borrow not the rules of my religion from Rome or Geneva, but the dictates of my own reason.'

However, we cannot capture him and call him ours. He was of his time. His thoughts are not our thoughts. He believed it was right to burn witches. He recorded in his commonplace book a cure for gout which required the application of tortoise-legs wrapped in the skin of a kid. He believed in the philosopher's stone which could turn base metal to gold.

In an age of bitter religious strife Thomas Browne's greatest achievement was to contribute to public debate more light than heat. He spoke and wrote with learning, eloquence and the gentle irony which wins affection and heals division.

WHAT IS PRAYER?

What is prayer? Try this: spend a few minutes to conjure up a scene or memory, a piece of music, a quarrel resolved or a friendship restored. Hold those thoughts, savour them and try to do so without verbalising. Just for a few moments, no more. What you are doing in this pause for reflection is common to all people. It is your response to a source of wonder outside yourself. It is the beginning of prayer.

That is all very well, you might think, but far too vague. True, but it is a starting point. So let us move forward and consider the idea (and practice) of Christian prayer. What is it that is different from the instinct shared by all human beings of every belief or none – a gasp of wonder at the glory of living, a cry of pain at the fear of dying?

At its deepest level prayer is silence, not words. It is the opening of the heart and mind to God in adoration; a simple, wordless, loving regard, which is both upwards to our Father in heaven and inwards to the ground of our being. As Meister Eckhart, the thirteenth-century German mystic, said, 'Nothing in all the world is so like God as stillness.' The difficulty is that few of us can achieve this simplicity. We are encumbered with too much mental baggage. The best we can do is to place ourselves before God just as we are, baggage and all. This will include random thoughts, joys, worries, sorrows, anger and, inevitably, remorse. We need at least some words to occupy our restless minds before we can be still.

Jesus taught his disciples to pray these words:

Our Father, who art in heaven, hallowed be thy Name.
Thy kingdom come. Thy will be done, on earth as it is in

ADRIAN LEAK

heaven. Give us this day our daily bread. And forgive us our
trespasses, as we forgive those who trespass against us. And
lead us not into temptation; but deliver us from evil.

The 'Our Father' (*Pater Noster* or Lord's Prayer) begins with
adoration, moves on to state our need, then asserts our
penitence and finally admits our dependence. It is a summary
of how to pray. It can be said quickly as a single prayer, or
slowly, each phrase being a peg on which to hang a period
of quiet reflection. It needs to be known by heart so that it
becomes part of our conscious and subconscious being. In
praying this prayer we are drawn into the mind of Christ
himself. They are his words.

Some people find it helpful to think of the four letters in the
word *acts* as being the initial letters of the four actions of prayer:
A for Adoration, *C* for Confession, *T* for Thanksgiving, *S* for
Supplication (asking). 'Asking' comes last, as it should, although
at times of stress or fear it is natural for us to put it first.

Adoration of God can be expressed in silent wonder, or in
brief phrases spoken from the heart. These can be addressed
directly to Our Lord Jesus Christ; it is easier to imagine his
human face responding to us with an affectionate smile, than
to envisage the invisible Father. *Lord Jesus, friend and brother,*
draw me closer to your heart of love.

Confession does not need to be an agonising exercise in
introspection or a list of faults, but a quiet acknowledgement
that we fall short of the person God wants us to be. In Jesus's
parable about the Pharisee and the Tax Collector (Luke 18:
9–14) it was enough for the tax collector simply to say 'Lord,
forgive me, a sinner', and to mean it. The danger of dwelling
upon our past faults is that it can stoke up the fires of guilt,
rather like scratching a sore. We come to God for healing, not
for punishment, and he knows better than us where the cause
of our sickness lies. *Lord Jesus, have mercy.*

Thanksgiving can be given for much more than what seems obvious: our family, our friends, our homes, our achievements, our talents. The Prayer Book's Prayer of General Thanksgiving says, 'We bless thee for our creation, preservation and all the blessings of this life, but above all for thine inestimable love in the redemption of the world by Our Lord Jesus Christ.' An expression of our gratitude can heal our peevish natures. *Thanks be to thee, my Lord Jesus Christ.*

Supplication (intercession) for ourselves or on behalf of others is the most frequently used part of prayer. It is natural that we should ask. Our Lord does not expect us to keep from him our worries or desires, whether they are great (a friend with cancer) or little (good weather for our holiday). If your anxiety has become a burden, place it at the foot of his cross and leave it there. *Lord, hear my prayer.*

The purpose of supplication is not simply to ask God to grant us, or the person we a praying for, a favour. When Jesus asked in the Garden of Gethsemane that the threat of suffering might be removed from him, he concluded his prayer with the words 'Nevertheless, not my will, but thine, be done'. The purpose of all prayer, including supplication, is to open ourselves to the will of God, not to bend his will to our advantage.

But, when all is said and done, words must give way to silence, as the Curé d'Ars discovered, when he encountered the old peasant, kneeling every day before the Blessed Sacrament in his church. 'What do you say to our Lord?' he asked. 'I say nothing,' the man replied. 'I look at him and he looks at me.'

GOD MEETS US IN THE DARK

(A sermon preached at St Alban's Church, Wood Street, Guildford,
at the Eucharist on the Fourth Sunday of Lent, 2003.)

Have you not known? Have you not heard? Have you not
understood? It is he who sits above the circle of the Earth, and
its inhabitants are like grasshoppers. It is he who stretched out
the heavens like a curtain... who brings princes to naught
and makes the rulers of the earth as nothing.
Lift up your eyes and see.

Isaiah 40: 21–23

There is a note of exasperation in the prophet's repeated
question:

Have you not known? Have you not heard? Have you not
understood? Why are the people being so stupid that they fail
to see what is there before their eyes? It is a recurring question
in the Bible: our inability to see the truth, to hear the truth and
to understand the truth.

Jesus's miracles of restoring sight to the blind, hearing to
the deaf and speech to the dumb were acts of compassion,
directed to individuals in their need. But the early disciples
saw in those miracles of healing a secondary meaning. They
were dramatic symbols, acted parables, teaching us that only
through God's grace can we see, hear and understand clearly
the truth of life.

When they came to write the story of Christ's saving deeds
in the Gospel, they wanted us to understand that an encounter
with the risen Lord can bring us closer to seeing the truth of

life, just as an encounter with Jesus brought sight and hearing to those blind and deaf people in Galilee.

Now I think that statement might be misleading. I do not believe that closeness to Christ – a strong personal faith – will help you or me to come up with any convincing answers to the questions which haunt us: 'Why so much suffering in this world? Why so much wickedness?'

A personal faith in God, however strong, will not answer those questions – will not solve the puzzle. We should be wary of any religious zealots who claim to know the answers.

I remember there used to be a soapbox orator in Hyde Park, at Speakers' Corner, whose message was quite simple, though he would deliver it in a terrifying rage. The answer to every possible question about life, the universe and everything was this: we had all sinned. We were all therefore doomed to burn in the flames of eternal punishment.

Once you grasped that simple truth, he said, everything else followed: he would then go through a catalogue of human tragedies – all those horrors which blight our existence, and which taken together create the human predicament: disease, infant mortality, famine, plane crashes, drought, floods, nuclear missiles. The list seemed endless. And he would punctuate his tirade with a bitter refrain: 'It's in the Book.' He would shout this, waving a bible above his head. 'You ask me how I know? I will tell you – *it's in the Book!* We are all doomed and we shall burn forever. *It's in the Book!*'

He would go on like this for a long time – getting angrier and angrier – then suddenly he would bring his tirade to an abrupt conclusion: 'You are all doomed and you shall burn forever… [pause]… Now if you'll excuse me, I have a bus to catch.' And he would be gone.

Prophets of doom often misuse the Bible, claiming to find in the words of Scripture support for their own distorted beliefs – beliefs in which anger and recrimination always play a bigger part than joy and forgiveness. But the overriding theme of the Bible is exactly the opposite to the doom-laden message of the Hyde Park preacher.

'Have you not known?' says Isaiah. 'Have you not heard? The Lord does not faint or grow weary. His understanding is unsearchable... Those who wait for the Lord shall mount up with wings like eagles... they shall run and not be weary, they shall walk and not faint.'

Now *there's* a message of hope if ever there was one. But the extraordinary thing was this: Isaiah was addressing these words to a depressed and broken community of Jewish exiles. There was nothing at all in the circumstances of their life to suggest anything other than gloom and despair.

Again and again in the Bible we are told that God will not abandon us. Again and again, both in the story of human experience and in the Bible, we hear of men and women refusing to be defeated by adversity. Their faith echoes the words of Job, who, in the midst of all his troubles, shouted his defiance: 'I know that my Redeemer liveth.'

These last ten days have been full of disaster:

A child killed by a falling tree in a Surrey school playground.
A student beaten to death as she walked home in Hampton.
A young American artist stabbed to death as she jogged in Victoria Park, Hackney.
A nineteen-year-old boy killed as he jumped from the top of a car park in Guildford.

And all the time the dark clouds of war are gathering on the horizon. We live in a dangerous world.*

God does not require us to turn our eyes away from the reality of darkness; to pretend that bad things are not

---

*   This was written in March 2003, a few days before the start of the Iraq War.

happening. Our Lord meets us in the dark, just as he encountered desolation upon the Cross. He calls us to stand firm in the faith of Isaiah and to declare with Job our belief that our Redeemer lives, and that, despite everything, he holds us, and will never, ever let us go.

DANCING ALONG DEATH'S ICY BRINK

Cease, Man, to mourn, to weep, to wail;
Enjoy thy shining hour of sun;
We dance along Death's icy brink,
But is the dance less full of fun?

Richard Burton 'Stanzas from the Kasidah'.

Well, yes, up to a point. But that kind of bravado doesn't really cut the mustard. Deep within our psyche there is this urge to treat death with a jokey flippancy. Confronted by the enormity of our impending extinction, we shrug our shoulders and turn aside with a casual quip. 'Die, my dear Doctor?' said Lord Palmerston on his death bed. 'That's the last thing I shall do.' And it was.

It is not surprising that we avert our eyes. At the crematorium the curtains close upon a reality too painful for to bear. At the graveside the handful of earth clatters noisily upon the coffin lid. The familiar words of committal spoken by the priest are stark and bitter: 'Earth to earth, ashes to ashes, dust to dust.' We hear the message, but we flinch at its meaning.

In fifteenth-century Paris a favourite meeting place and promenade was the churchyard of Holy Innocents. The surrounding cloister accommodated a number of charnel houses, depositories for the skulls and bones of corpses which had been exhumed to make room to receive the recent dead. In spite of the daily burials and exhumations, the churchyard was a popular rendezvous. Market stalls did a busy trade, friends chatted, lovers kept tryst, deals were done, prostitutes touted for business. Looking down upon this scene from the cloister walls was a lugubrious mural depicting the *Danse Macabre*, with Death, a capering cadaver, guiding the dancers down to the grave. The citizens of Paris saw the message but chose to dodge its truth.

Of all people Christians should learn to look death in the face. It is only in the dark that we can see the glorious light. Our belief is this: that between Christ's death on the Friday and his rising at dawn on the Sunday his body lay dead in the tomb. His death was real; it was no pretence. The curtains of mortality were drawn close. The iron gates clanged shut. There was a discontinuity – a great and universal hiatus when God, even the Lord himself, died, and all Creation held her breath.

Death is death, and we and all those we love, our friends, our families, our children, our pets, our neighbours, all chance acquaintances, all those we have not known and those we will never know, all members of this human race, past, present and those yet to come, all creatures of our terrestrial world, and not only they, but the entire universe which has existed since the dawn of time, when the *morning stars sang together* and *the sons of God shouted for joy*, all are destined to one certain and unimaginable end.

But that is not the end. In dying Christ took death into eternal life. On Easter morning he rose again and broke asunder the fetters of time. Drawing aside the curtains of mortality, the Lord of the Dance now leads the great company of creation, redeemed by his conquering love, through the wide-open gates to a timeless and eternal realm where:

The ransomed of the Lord shall return with singing. Sorrow and sighing shall flee away.

Isaiah 35: 10

THE MAN WHO PAVED PICCADILLY

John Evelyn
1620–1706
Diarist

(Extracted from an article first published in
the *Church Times*, February 2006.)

After an evening with his fellow diarist John Evelyn, Samuel Pepys wrote, 'I never met with so merry a two hours as our company that night was… Mr Evelyn repeating some verses… did make us all die almost with laughing.' Pepys qualified his opinion on another occasion by writing, 'In fine a most excellent person he is and must be allowed a little for a little conceitedness; but he may well be so, being a man so much above others.'

Evelyn's diary is driven by an egregious curiosity. He studied chemistry in Paris and anatomy in Padua. He observed the pelican in St James's Park and measured its beak. He gives us a detailed account of the first rhinoceros to be brought into this country and tells us how he placed his hand into the mouth of a tame lion in order to feel the roughness of its tongue. He describes for us the stork which stumped about St James's Park on a wooden leg. In the same park plane trees, ancestors of the ones there today, were planted on his advice to purify London's polluted air.

He tells us how as a young man on his grand tour he visited the Pope. 'I was presented to kiss his toe, that is, his embroidered slipper, two cardinals holding up his vest and surplice, and then being sufficiently blessed with his thumb and two fingers, I returned home to dinner.'

At a time when the life of the nation was dislocated by the Civil War, Evelyn and other like-minded men and women carried on as best they could. Discreetly, in the universities and in the libraries of their country houses, they trimmed the lamps of science and art, and kept them burning against better times.

The Anglican Church, now proscribed by parliament, went underground. And so did those scholars, architects, priests and musicians who were to lead the renaissance of science, music, literature, art and religion at the Restoration in 1660. There was one place where they found collective asylum: Oxford.

Evelyn's diary gives us glimpses of this state of cultural hibernation during the bleak years of the Commonwealth. In the autumn of 1654 he took his young wife to visit friends in Oxford. They had dinner with the Professor of Mathematics, Dr Seth Ward (later Bishop of Salisbury). The next evening they were invited to a 'magnificent entertainment' in Wadham College by Evelyn's 'excellent and dear friend' the Warden, Dr John Wilkins (later Bishop of Chester). The following evening there was a concert in All Souls College where some 'ingenious scholars' sang to the accompaniment of 'theorboes'. A theorbo was a double-necked lute, an instrument which Evelyn himself had studied in Italy. The following day they visited the Bodleian Library where they met the librarian Thomas Barlow (later, Bishop of Lincoln) who showed them some of its treasures, including Arabic and Greek manuscripts.

At All Souls College they met the young mathematician and astronomer Christopher Wren, with whom Evelyn was later appointed by Charles II to conduct a detailed survey of Old St Paul's. London's cathedral had reached an advanced state of dilapidation. Before the Civil War Inigo Jones had remodelled the west front to a classical design. In 1666 Evelyn and Wren followed Inigo Jones's classical lead and, against strong opposition, recommended the replacement of the crumbling spire with a dome. A week later the entire cathedral was destroyed in the Great Fire, and Wren's plans were eventually adopted.

It was in Oxford and as early as 1648 that the Royal Society had its genesis. Evelyn, who was a founder member, refers in his diary to the *junto*, or club, of academics and literati, who met informally in Dr Wilkins's rooms at Wadham College to discuss 'experimental philosophy' (the natural sciences).

Soon after the death of Oliver Cromwell – Evelyn said that 'It was the joyfullest funeral I ever saw, for there were none that cried, but dogs' – King Charles II was restored to the throne and appointed him Commissioner for Improving London's Streets. Evelyn ordered the paving of the quagmire called *Pigudillo* (Piccadilly).

They were all one to an enquiring mind – the pelican, the rhinoceros, the plane trees, the embroidered slipper, the arrangement of the papal fingers in a gesture of blessing. Evelyn, the devout Anglican, was also the detached and scientific observer, standing at the threshold of the Age of Reason.

In retirement he returned to his beloved Surrey. His elder brother had died, leaving to him the Wotton estate. Here he lived out his remaining years amongst his books and gardens, and attending to the family and the social responsibilities of a country gentleman. Central to his life was the practice of his Christian faith. He read his bible, said his prayers, attended his parish church, listened critically to the sermons (though, as age took hold, he sometimes fell asleep), and received regularly with great devotion, and only after due preparation, the holy sacrament.

THE HAND THAT ROCKS THE CRADLE

Mary Sumner
1828–1921
Founder of the Mothers' Union

(First published in the *Church Times*, August 2005.)

For the hand that rocks the cradle
Is the hand that rules the world.

William Ross Wallace 1819–1881

When George and Mary Sumner drove away from their wedding in her father's best carriage, the postilions wore white favours for the bride. It was the start of a great partnership.

They belonged by birth and breeding to the evangelical tradition of piety, wealth and philanthropy. It was in the blood. Mary, born in 1828, had grown up in a mansion, with peacocks on the lawn and daily prayers in the hall – a lifestyle fuelled by banking and driven by godliness. George's family background included William Wilberforce and Henry Thornton.

When they moved into the Rectory at Old Alresford, they brought an unfamiliar earnestness to the parish. The previous incumbent, Lord Guilford, had been an absentee, whose rare visits (in a four-in-hand with earl's coronet on the carriage door) had never failed to surprise the parish.

During the thirty-four years of their residence the Sumners transformed church life. Mary helped her husband visit the cottages and catechise the children. She welcomed parishioners to her drawing room, sang Handel's arias in the village reading room, trained the choir and played the church organ.

Remembering how she had felt when she had held her first-born, she said, 'It struck me how much I needed special training for so great a work and how little I knew.' In 1876 she called a gathering of local mothers at the rectory. The ladies who had arrived in carriages mingled with the 'cottage mothers' who had walked. They were addressed first by the Rector about the duties of Christian motherhood, and then by his wife.

In no other venue than a rectory drawing room could a meeting so diverse have taken place; and by none other than a Mary Sumner could the ladies in gloves be told, in the presence of the women in bonnets, that the wealthy as well as the poor might need instruction. Nevertheless, she respected the social divisions. There were, for example, two sorts of membership card, one for the 'lady mothers' who paid a subscription, and the other for 'cottage mothers' who did not. In the printed membership cards offering domestic guidance, avoidance of beer and coarse jests was enjoined upon the cottage mothers, but tactfully omitted from the cards given to the lady mothers.

In 1885 Mary Sumner was persuaded to address the Church Congress at Portsmouth. 'What can be done to raise the national character?' she asked. 'Let us appeal to the mothers of England... Those who rock the cradle rule the world.' The Mothers' Union was on its way.

Her early training helped. As a singer she knew how to project her voice at public rallies. Her stamina and courage carried her through a punishing schedule. She was no stranger to peril. She travelled frequently, often in storms, and once at the gallop through the cholera-ridden streets of St Jean de Luz, her handkerchief held to her face. She was once stranded halfway up the Great Pyramid, and on another occasion was thrown by her mule into a Palestinian stream. She visited the harems of Damascus and persuaded the men of Alresford to give presents to their wives.

She became – or, rather, had never ceased to be – a *grande dame*. Not an aristocrat, but tougher: a daughter of the late Georgian *haute bourgeoisie*. In old age she commented upon the author Charlotte Yonge's shabby dress at an MU rally: 'A social dereliction,' she said. She remained incorrigibly and gloriously of her class and of her time.

RICHARD HOOKER AND THE *VIA MEDIA*

1554–1600
Scholar, Priest and Apologist for the Anglican *Via Media*

(First published in the *Church Times*, November 2000.)

When Hooker's young pupils, George Cranmer and Edwyn Sandys, travelled from Oxford in 1584 to visit him in his new parish of Drayton Beauchamp, they were dismayed to find their master in a field, tending sheep and reading a small volume of Horace's *Odes*. They did not consider this to be the proper conduct of a serious theologian.

They were even more upset when they went indoors and had their conversation frequently interrupted by his wife, Joan, who insisted that he rock the baby's cradle instead of talking divinity with his friends. Anthony à Wood, the Oxford antiquarian, described her as a clownish and silly woman, but there is no evidence that the marriage was unhappy and Hooker spoke of her lovingly to the end of his life.

Matrimony was still a novel status for the clergy, and society was unsure how to regard the clergy wife. The Queen disapproved: 'Madam I may not call you; mistress I am ashamed to call you; and so I know not what to call you,' she said to the wife of the Archbishop of Canterbury in one of the greatest put-downs of all time (*what* would Mrs Proudie have done?). Some of that edgy resentment in the presence of a clergy wife is betrayed by Hooker's bachelor friends, who later put it about that Hooker's choice of wife could only be explained by his poor eyesight. Years later George Cranmer was still repeating this *canard*, and it found its way into Izaak Walton's *Life of Hooker*.

Hooker was one of the first of a long line of Anglican theologians who have had to put down their books to do the washing up, rock the cradle or mow the lawn; scholars who, in Walton's romantic vision, 'Have been drawn from the tranquillity of [their] college, from that garden of piety... and sweet conversation, into the thorny wilderness of a busy world; into those corroding cares that attend a married priest and a country parsonage.'

He was a country parson for much of his career – at Drayton Beauchamp in Buckinghamshire, at Boscombe in Wiltshire, and then finally at Bishopsbourne in Kent, where his monument describes him as 'Judicious'. He possessed one of the finest minds of his generation and wrote his *Laws of Ecclesiastical Polity*, not in the solitude of a university study but amongst the contingencies of parish life.

Others followed in this tradition and have given Anglican piety its characteristically pastoral and pragmatic flavour. Among his contemporaries was Lancelot Andrewes, and in the following generation were George Herbert, John Cosin, Jeremy Taylor and Thomas Ken. The line is a long and distinguished one. It descends to our own day when there is still to be found a small number of Anglican scholars, on the bench of bishops and in our vicarages, who have chosen to leave the academic life to 'do their theology' in parish or diocese.

Hooker did not cut prepossessing figure. Walton describes him as –

> 'an obscure harmless man; a man in poor clothes, his loins usually girt in a coarse gown or canonical coat; of a mean stature and stooping, and yet more lowly in the thoughts of his soul; his body worn out not with age, but with study and mortifications; his face full of heat pimples, begot by his inactivity and sedentary life'.

He was, however, sufficiently active as a parish priest to earn the affection of his flock, and his humility was well known. A familiar sight to the parishioners was their vicar and the parish clerk, each struggling to doff his hat before the other. 'Dove-like in his simplicity' was how one contemporary described him. Yet this was the man of whom, at his death Lancelot Andrewes said, 'He hath not left any near him.' During his lifetime his fame reached Rome. When Pope Clement VIII heard part of the first book of *The Laws of Ecclesiastical Polity* read to him in Latin, he said, 'There is no learning that this man hath not searched into; nothing is too hard for his understanding,' and he ordered that the rest of the work be translated.

Hooker's legacy to Anglicanism is so rich, and the extent to which our thinking has been shaped by him so great, that it is hard to find any of our attitudes which do not bear his mark. The ubiquity of his influence renders it almost invisible.

At the time he wrote – towards the end of Elizabeth I's reign – the prevailing mood of the Church of England was strongly Calvinist. Those features of the Elizabethan Settlement which subsequently seemed so well established – the Book of Common Prayer and the three-fold Ordained Ministry – were under severe threat from the Puritan party. Popular opinion was growing impatient with a church which appeared, in its liturgy and orders, to be closer to Rome than to the Continental reformers. To defend the Settlement merely on the grounds that it avoided the opposing extremes of Rome and Geneva seemed a feeble argument, and yet that appeared to be its only defence.

Hooker's achievement was to give the Anglican Church a rationale, integrity and authority which was distinctively its own, but which was at the same time continuous with the pre-Reformation Catholic Church, descended from the Church of Anselm and the Church of the Fathers. It was this achievement which allowed Thomas Ken to say, as he lay dying a century later:

*I die in the Holy Catholic and Apostolic Faith, professed
by the whole Church before the disunion of East and West.
More particularly I die in the Communion of the Church of
England as it stands distinguished from all Papal and Puritan
innovations and as it adheres to the doctrine of the Cross.*

His *Laws of Ecclesiastical Polity* engage at different levels. At his
loftiest he propounds the view that truth cannot be determined
by an appeal to Scripture alone but must be sought with the
aid of human reason and perceived in natural law as well
as revelation. His attack upon the notion that truth can be
encompassed within and authenticated by a closed theological
system undermined both the Roman and Puritan positions,
and was all the more devastating for its reasonableness.

He applied the same reasoning to the development of civil
institutions as to ecclesiastical. He did not believe it possible to
defend the existence of any particular secular authority without
recourse to arguments based upon expediency, and what might
be perceived as the working of natural law in primitive society.
The notion of kings ruling by divine right had no place in his
philosophy. In that respect he was a precursor of Hobbes and
Locke.

Over the contentious issue of the Real Presence of our
Lord in the elements of the Eucharist, he wrote:

*What these elements are in themselves it skilleth not; it is
enough that to me which take them they are the Body and
Blood of Christ... Why should any cogitation possess the
mind of the faithful communicant but this, 'O my God, thou
art true. O my soul, thou art happy.'*

In a generation which was quick to consign its theological
opponents to eternal damnation – 'no Papist can be saved' was
the burden of many a sermon – Hooker's generosity of spirit

was thought to be a sign of weakness. But he could not bring himself, he said, to write upon the graves of those who held erroneous views: 'Such men are damned; there is for them no salvation.' In a moving passage he wrote:

> *Give me a Pope or Cardinal... whose heart God hath touched with true sorrow for all his sins, and filled with the love of Christ and his Gospel... shall I think... such men touch not the hem of Christ's garment?*

Hooker defended the Book of Common Prayer against those who would abolish it in favour of a less structured liturgy. Its formularies, he argued, were the laity's protection against the whims of preachers and the undisciplined longueurs of an ignorant clergy. He reminded his readers that in its provision of a balanced and integrated system of worship, which included the Daily Office, the Eucharist, the Occasional Offices, Kalendar and Lectionary, they possessed in a single volume a unique compendium of the Christian life.

He appealed to reason and common sense over those subjects of religious dispute which he admitted were too trivial for serious debate. For example, on the question of whether to stand or sit during the reading of the Gospel – a subject which was hotly disputed at the time – he wrote:

> *'Now because the Gospels... do all historically declare something which our Lord Jesus Christ himself either spake, did or suffered in his own person, it hath been the custom of Christian men then especially in token of the greater reverence to stand, to utter certain words of acclamation, and at the name of Jesus to bow the head. Which harmless ceremonies, as there is no man constrained to use, so we know no reason wherefore any man should yet imagine it an unsufferable evil.'*

He introduced into the anger of theological debate a disarmingly simple manner, which was enough to deflate the furious rhetoric of his opponents. Reading some of his words, you can almost see his cocked eyebrow as he seems to be saying, 'Come now, let us look at this matter calmly and sensibly, and see if we cannot come to an honest resolution.'

There is nothing in what his contemporaries wrote to suggest that he had a great sense of humour – at least, not in the obvious sense – but hidden in the text of his work are scintillas of wit which sparkle on the page. In referring to the terrifyingly irascible St Jerome, he comments with the gentlest irony that his 'custom is not to pardon over easily his adversaries if anywhere they chance to trip'.

Although Swift claimed that Hooker had written so naturally that his English had survived all changes of fashion our own generation, with its fear of the subordinate clause, would find his prose uncomfortable to read. According to Thomas Fuller, the seventeenth-century historian, 'his style was long and pithy, driving a whole flock of clauses before he comes to the close of a sentence'. Even in his own day his style was not to everyone's taste. Some of his parishioners found his preaching 'perplext, tedious and obscure' and 'his voice low, his stature little, gesture none at all, standing stone-still in the pulpit'.

Even so, as we celebrate the fourth centenary of the death of this 'obscure, harmless man', we can only stand in wonder at the incalculable effect he had upon the English Reformation. Not only did his scholarship define the Anglican Church, but his sanctity of life, his humility and sweet temperament set a new and lasting standard for religious debate and clerical conduct.

JOHN MILTON: ALBION'S VIRGIL

1608–1674

(First published in the *Church Times* in May 2008.)

'Madam,' said Dr Johnson, 'Milton was a genius that could cut a Colossus from a rock; but could not carve heads upon cherry-stones.' Not, perhaps, quite fair, but close enough. The impression that Milton himself wished to make upon his contemporaries, and to leave posterity, was one of grandeur and genius. He was England's Homer, Albion's Virgil. His high opinion of himself was a view shared by few at the time, but by many in the succeeding centuries.

> *Greece sound thy Homer's, Rome thy Virgil's name,*
> *But England's Milton equals both in fame.*

> William Cowper 1731–1800

It is the reputation that repels. The apparent solemnity and colossal volume of the one work by which he is most widely known, *Paradise Lost*, has probably lost more potential readers in our generation than would otherwise have delighted in the lyricism, say, of *L'Allegro* and *Il Penseroso*, the majesty of *On the Morning of Christ's Nativity* and the elegiac beauty of *Lycidas*.

Behind the public face of England's self-appointed Virgil was a passionate man, whose private feelings break cover again and again. He could not have written about the pleasures of youth so convincingly and with such lightness of touch had he not first enjoyed them:

Haste thee, Nymph, and bring with thee
Jest, and youthful Jollity,
Quips and cranks and wanton wiles,
Nods and becks and wreathéd smiles…
Come, and trip it as you go
On the light fantastic toe.

L'Allegro

He could never have written so movingly about the desolation of bereavement had he not known the intensity of human love. In his sonnet *On His Deceased Wife* he tells how in a dream 'Methought I saw my late espoused wife' and goes on to describe how he sees her standing beside him. The verse moves upwards to a climax of joy, before crashing in the final line upon ten sharp rocks of pain:

to my fancied sight
Love, sweetness, goodness, in her person shined
So clear as in no face with more delight,
But, oh! as to embrace me she inclined,
I waked, she fled and day brought back my night.

Although there is a note of serene resignation in his sonnet *On His Blindness* ('They also serve who only stand and wait'), no one can read the lines about Samson's blindness in *Samson Agonistes* without hearing in them the poet's shout of rage and pain at his own terrible affliction:

O dark, dark, dark, amid the blaze of noon,
Irrecoverably dark, total eclipse
Without all hope of day!

How could a man who could reveal such raw emotion have won a reputation for cool detachment? The answer must be that he himself wished it so. In his own words he admitted to 'a certain niceness of nature, an honest haughtiness'. He was never in any doubt about his superior talents. Why should he be, when the evidence was so clear? He had, after all, read all the poetry written in his native tongue, most of the works of Greek and Latin antiquity, was fluent in French and Italian, and was familiar with the poetry of both those languages.

No wonder he scorned the efforts of his fellow undergraduates at Christ's College, Cambridge, as they presented their college plays in Latin. 'While they acted, and over-acted... they thought themselves gallant men, and I thought them fools; they made sport and I laughed; they mispronounced and I misliked.' He called them buffoons; they called him 'The Lady of Christ's College', in allusion to his beauty and fastidious nature.

When at the age of twenty-one he completed *On the Morning of Christ's Nativity*, he knew that he had written a great work. To have pretended otherwise would have been a denial of the gift God had bestowed. At the age of twenty-five, in response to his father's questioning about what he meant to do with his life – there had been a lot of a sitting about at home, reading books – Milton composed a Latin poem, *Ad Patrem*, in which he declared that it was his vocation to be a poet, and one whose destiny was not to walk with the crowd but to wear the laureate's crown.

Milton's God was not only the bounteous creator who had been generous in his benefactions but was also the poet's taskmaster. Driven by the knowledge that he must make proper use of these gifts, Milton searched and waited for a worthy subject. In the years 1639–41 he was considering the composition of a great epic poem, and made lists of possible subjects, some from the Bible, some from our history. He drafted the outline of a poem about the Fall of Man. For many years he hardly wrote a verse. Then in 1658 he started to write *Paradise Lost*.

The opening invocation at the start of his great epic has echoes of the opening lines of the *Aeneid*. In place of Virgil's 'Of arms and the man I sing...' Milton begins:

> *Of man's first disobedience and the fruit*
> *Of that forbidden tree whose mortal taste*
> *Brought death into the world...*

The muse whom Milton invokes is not one of the sacred nine, but the:

> *Heavenly Muse, that on the secret top*
> *Of Oreb, or of Sinai didst inspire*
> *That shepherd who first taught the chosen seed...*

In other words, Moses's muse, the Holy Spirit.

The use of a model like the Aeneid, and the frequent references to classical mythology in Milton's work, were not just literary conceits. Nor were they, as they would later become when employed by writers in the nineteenth century, a tiresome display of erudition and classical learning. In the seventeenth century they expressed the current belief, developed by the Cambridge neoplatonists, that the poets and philosophers of Greece and Rome, together with the Hebrew prophets, were channels of God's self-disclosure. Plato was 'the Attic Moses', and according to Ralph Cudworth, the Professor of Hebrew at Cambridge University at that time, 'Pythagoras drew his knowledge from the Hebrew fountains', and Plato his from Pythagoras.

It was a line of thought that was to lead eventually to the latitudinarianism which became so marked a feature of the

Church of England in the eighteenth century, and which in a developed form dispensed with the doctrine of the Trinity altogether. It was more Stoic than Christian. Benjamin Whichcote, Provost of King's College during Milton's time at Cambridge, and a popular preacher, said, 'Give me religion that is grounded in reason... The religion that makes men courteous, affable and sociable, not sour, morose and dogged; that makes me ready to forgive, not implacable.'

It was, like Milton's, a religion that preached salvation by obedience, reason, virtue, qualities of which Jesus was the supreme exemplar. There was very little room for Christ's atoning sacrifice. It was a religion of merit, not grace. In *Paradise Regained* the cosmic battle between good and evil is fought in the Judaean wilderness, not on Calvary, and Christ emerges as the victor after the third temptation.

There were good reasons why Milton should have turned to this reasonable version of Christianity, when the other versions could be so unappealing. The Laudian party, which stressed the Catholic heritage of the Church of England, was, in Milton's eyes, disfigured by the character and conduct of its two leading figures: Archbishop Laud and King Charles I. The Puritan party, with its ranting and rancour, was discredited by men like Prynne who said that, 'The Apostles and the Christians of the primitive church were for the most part weepers, not laughers.' Prynne was much against masques and stage plays, especially those which made people laugh: 'Christ Jesus our pattern was always mourning, not laughing; I am sure not at a stage play.'

Much has been said about Milton's portrayal of Satan. He certainly comes close to being the hero of *Paradise Lost* and, like the seductively charming Comus he has the best lines. Blake's words that Milton 'was in fetters when he wrote of angels and God, and at liberty when of devils and hell, because he was a true poet, and of the devil's party without knowing it', are ones with which Milton may have agreed. He might, perhaps, have replied – and this may have been what Blake meant – that a consequence of the Fall must be the poet's inability to depict evil as less compelling than good, and in a poem about the Fall written by a creature of the Fall, Satan must inevitably be a charmer.

There was another role which Milton played. It was one which called from his pen some of the noblest prose written in the English language – and some of the worst. 'Worst', not because those passages were ill-written or dull, but because they were distorted by malice, and demeaned the writer more than they damaged their victims.

Milton was a polemicist and pamphleteer, a fighter for civil liberties far ahead of his time. Rose Macaulay described his prose 'Flinging up huge sentences, like baroque palaces, to the sky', but she deplored 'the coarse brutality'. In *The Tenure of Kings and Magistrates* he defended the state's right to depose and execute a tyrant; in *The Doctrine and Discipline of Divorce* he argued in favour of divorce on the grounds of irretrievable breakdown; in his *Areopagitica* he wrote passionately in defence of a free press.

It was in this last work, addressed to Parliament in 1643, that his prose rose to its greatest heights. It is true, however, that Milton did get carried away with his own eloquence, describing a country gloriously free at a time when it was close to anarchy. He concluded with the famous peroration: that ours is, 'a nation not slow and dull, but of a quick, ingenious and piercing spirit... methinks I see in my mind a noble and puissant nation rousing herself like a strong man after sleep, and shaking her invincible locks. Methinks I see her as an eagle mewing her mighty youth.' In 1643 that was, sadly, very far from the truth, but it was a noble vision.

But it was in his series of pamphlets attacking episcopacy that his prose descended to the depths of lampoonery. He had not always been so hostile; in 1626 he had written an elegy on the death of Lancelot Andrewes. Now he wrote sneeringly of the bishops in their 'deformed and fantastic dresses in palls, and mitres, gold and gewgaws fetched from Aaron's old wardrobe'. In response, an opponent alleged that at Cambridge Milton had spent his time 'loitering, bezelling and harlotting'. For his part, Milton said that one of the bishops had smelly feet. Such exchanges were the stuff of theological debate, but it was surprising to find Milton involved.

During this fourth centenary year of John Milton's birth, how do we best serve his memory? Surely not by trying to smooth away unsightly wrinkles from the reputation of a great man. His achievement was, to use Dr Johnson's word, colossal. His poetry and his prose reached soaring heights of beauty. His arrogance was heroic. His vision of civil and domestic liberty was such that Wordsworth's cry 'Milton! Thou should'st be living at this hour' is one which every generation must make their own.

But he too was human, and blemished; at times silly, at times malicious; but despite all that, despite his *hauteur*, he belongs to all of us, to that vast crowd of men and women, not only in England, but in every land where people have inherited as their own the language he spoke and the principles of liberty for which he fought.

QUEEN ANNE'S BOUNTY

(First published in the *Church Times*, 8 March 2002.)

Swift wrote that an English country parson possessed of a house and barn in good repair, a field or two to graze his cows, and a garden and orchard, could live 'like an honest plain farmer'. Few country clergy at that time would have been so sanguine. In 1716 the incumbent of Osbornby complained about his benefice income, 'I have not made above £12 this year, it consisting chiefly in wool and lamb, and there having been such a rot both last year and this that I know not how I shall subsist.'

The clergy themselves were not the only people to be worried. There was, in the early years of the eighteenth century, a general feeling that the poverty of the parson was bringing the church into contempt. His attempts to supplement his earnings by taking in pupils only led later to even greater ridicule in Rowlandson's series of caricatures of the parson-schoolteacher, *Dr Syntax*.

On a living of less than £50 a year a parson was unable to purchase books, maintain his robes, buy new clothes for himself and his family, or even pay the butcher's and the baker's bills. He cut a sorry figure in the neighbourhood. For want of educated society and reading, his conversation grew dull and his sermons worse. Gilbert Burnet, Bishop of Salisbury, had warned William III of the consequences of this decline: 'A poor clergy may be scandalous, but must be both ignorant and contemptible.'

Queen Anne set aside an annual income of £17,000 out of the Crown revenues to augment the poorer benefices. The figure in the values of that time was large and generous. However, her ministers saw the gift as politically shrewd – a means of buying the loyalty of the lower clergy who were troublesome and Tory, unlike their bishops who were bland and Whig.

The source of this part of the royal income was the ancient ecclesiastical tax of First Fruits and Tenths. Originally this had been levied on the English clergy by the Pope. Each incumbent had to pay a proportion of his first year's income (the First Fruits), and thereafter a smaller and annually recurring charge (the Tenths). Henry VIII had diverted these taxes into his own treasury, but neither he nor his successors had used the revenue for ecclesiastical purposes. After the Restoration the revenue from First Fruits and Tenths was used, amongst other things, for the upkeep of the royal mistresses and the maintenance of a secret service.

This fund, designated for the augmentation of poor livings, became known as Queen Anne's Bounty. First from a building next to the Banqueting Hall in Whitehall, then from their offices in Dean's Yard, the governors of the bounty discharged their trust from 1704 until 1948, when they were merged with the Ecclesiastical Commission to form the Church Commissioners.

To begin with they saw their task as a simple one of diverting funds from the wealthier to the poorer clergy. Incumbents of livings worth over £50 a year were taxed on the old basis of First Fruits and Tenths. This yielded an annual average of £17,000 for distribution, in the first place, to livings worth less than £10, later to those less than £50. In fact, the amount the bounty office received was usually less than £14,000, because the money had to pass through the exchequer which was responsible for collection and extracted its own fees.

The governors of Queen Anne's Bounty were prudent trustees: they insisted that augmentation should be in the form of capital endowment rather than an annual gift of cash.

The poorest livings were chosen by lot to receive an endowment of a maximum value of £200. The incumbents were then required to purchase land or tithes up to that value and this, it was calculated, would raise their benefice income by £10 a year.

It was a laborious and cautious method of disbursement. It placed upon the individual clergyman the burden of finding an appropriate piece of land and then negotiating with the vendor – a process which sometimes took years to complete.

More successful was the bounty's policy of attracting additional gifts from lay benefactors to match their own. The governors announced that if the local squire or patron was willing to endow the living with property in the form of land or tithes, the bounty would match this up to the value of £200. To begin with there was a healthy response from patrons wishing to enhance the value of their advowsons.

Lady Thorold told the governors:

> *I will settle £40 a year upon Siston living, that with the £13 a year which Sir John always paid the minister, will make the living £53 a year, which will be maintenance for a single man – and I desire he shall preach once every Sunday and read prayers twice every Sunday.*

However, Queen Anne's simple attempt to support her poorest clergy had far from simple consequences.

Not everyone wished to see this growth in church property. Alienation of land from lay ownership into the hands of the clergy aroused the landed gentry's latent suspicions. Lord Egremont recorded in his diary in 1730 the conversation at his table: 'We talked of Queen Anne's act for the augmentation of livings, which most of the company said would prove of dangerous consequence in the end.' And correspondents to the *Gentleman's Magazine* (which served much the same purpose in the eighteenth century as do the correspondence columns of the *Daily Telegraph* in our own day) painted an improbable picture of predatory clergy who in their greed for legacies battened upon vulnerable parishioners, 'watching the last moments of dying persons, as insidiously as ever the monks and friars did in the darkest times of popery and superstition'.

The parson, it was thought, was all very well so long as he kept his place, which was higher than that of the people, but considerably lower than that of the squire. His job was to preserve the established order of society by reminding the tenants of their duty to God and their landlord. That, put crudely, is how Parliament understood the role of the established church.

Lady Thorold's requirements of her parson in return for her donation reflect the attitude of her time. As does Addison's *alter ego*, the genial Worcestershire squire Sir Roger de Coverley, who, having supplied his church with hassocks so that his tenants might kneel and prayer books so that they might recite the psalms, engaged the services of an itinerant musician to teach them how to sing, and then appointed 'his chaplain' on the understanding that he must never attempt to preach his own sermons, but use instead those from published collections.

Given those attitudes – appropriate to that age – it is not surprising that the church's attempts to improve its resources and efficiency should have been viewed as a threat. The greater attention now being urged by archdeacons to accuracy in keeping church *terriers* – no more than the sort of basic inventory which any lay landowner would regard as fundamental to efficient management – was seen by many as an act of clerical aggression. It was bad enough that the church should be a landlord, but to aspire to be an efficient landlord was insupportable.

Parliament acted swiftly, and in 1736 passed an act restricting the amount of land which could be transferred by private gift to the church. This embargo was lifted in 1803, and the church's progress towards solvency – if not affluence – was able to continue unhindered by the gentry. The effect of this was to accelerate the gentrification of the parsonage, a process which led to the founding of the great clerical families which dominated the Victorian church.

Another unforeseen consequence of Queen Anne's benefaction was to enhance the influence of lay patrons. Clearly, it was more desirable to be the patron of a living worth £50 than one worth £10. In an age when patronage was a social – even a commercial – asset, the possession of the advowson of an enhanced living not only benefited the owner but strengthened the whole system of private patronage. It also preserved depopulated parishes from pastoral re-organisation.

Early in the history of the bounty, complaints were being made by some of the bishops that the governors used poverty as the only criterion for selecting livings for augmentation. Differences in workload or population were not considered. Archbishop Tenison wanted the governors to distinguish between active and lazy parsons. Wake (Lincoln) wanted many of the poorest livings to be merged rather than augmented. He urged his brother bishops to draw up lists of benefices which might benefit from union, and to persuade Parliament to pass a comprehensive act to bring this about. Nothing came of the idea.

Later, the governors began to attach conditions to their disbursements: workload was taken into account; clergy were to reside in their parishes; they were to take at least one service each Sunday. These requirements were also imposed upon those clergy who had applied for loans to assist them with the repair or rebuilding of the parsonage.

Repairs to the parsonage ('dilapidations') were frequently a heavy burden upon a newly appointed incumbent. Legally the outgoing incumbent was liable for dilapidations. This was no comfort to the new man if his predecessor was dead, bankrupt or mad – and nearly every new incumbent was faced with one or other of these situations. In many parishes the parsonage had simply disappeared or fallen into ruin, the services being taken by a visiting curate.

When he was shown the parsonage at Badsey, his new living in the Vale of Evesham, George Drummond declared that it was no more than a weaver's hovel and ordered the building of a new one. He was lucky; he could afford to pay for this out of his own pocket. Few were so fortunate. Most had to apply to Queen Anne's Bounty for a mortgage, thereby encumbering the living with a debt which might take years to clear.

Again there were unforeseen consequences. It was not enough simply to pay out money. Control and intervention were needed, and it was not long before the governors were able to enforce a survey on each benefice house as the living fell vacant and application for funds was made. From being simply a channel of funds to the poorer livings, the governors found themselves acting as a central monitor both of clerical conduct and of benefice property.

By the end of the First World War the Ecclesiastical Commissioners (founded in 1835) had taken over from Queen Anne's Bounty responsibility for augmentation, the income from First Fruits and Tenths having dwindled to practically nothing and ceasing altogether in 1926. Thereafter the bounty was occupied with the painfully controversial business of collecting and distributing tithe rent charges, until the abolition of tithes in 1936. Its remaining duty was to act as the central authority for parsonage dilapidations, which it administered through the dioceses. Finally, in 1948, the bounty was wound up and was merged with the Ecclesiastical Commissioners to become the Church Commissioners.

There can be no doubt that over the two and a half centuries of its independent existence Queen Anne's Bounty served the church well, fulfilling, in part at least, its original purpose of augmenting the poorest livings, and of attracting considerable private wealth for the maintenance of parish clergy. What is not so clear is whether in doing so it was acting as an engine of change or preserver of the *status quo*. Perhaps it did both – which, after all, was appropriate, considering the character and position of its royal founder.

DR JOHNSON

1709–1784
Conversationalist, Writer and Lexicographer

(First published in the *Church Times*, December 2003.)

Despite his great lumbering physique, robust appetite and hearty delight in good company, Dr Johnson was afflicted throughout his life by ill health, deafness, severely impaired vision, disfigurement and recurring bouts of depression. Added to these disabilities were the inner demons which rarely ceased to torment his spirit: a sense of his own moral failure, a fear of insanity and, worst of all, a terror that for all the assurance of the Christian creed life might, after all, be meaningless as well as miserable. It was this last which prompted him to ask:

> *Must helpless man, in ignorance sedate,*
> *Roll darkling down the torrent of his fate?*

> (The Vanity of Human Wishes)

This is not how we usually think of him. He has given us a different picture of himself. 'A tavern chair is the throne of felicity,' he said. 'Wine there exhilarates my spirits, and prompts those I most love; I dogmatise and am contradicted, and in this conflict of opinions and sentiments I find delight.' It is the familiar picture of the 'Great Cham of English literature', the one we know from Boswell's *Life*: clubbable, much-loved by his friends, full of practical wisdom, irascible and sometimes devastatingly rude, but more often charitable and tender, a man at ease in his world, secure in his fame and at peace with himself.

The facts were otherwise. Far from enjoying a carefree life of conviviality and good cheer, Johnson was a deeply troubled man, conscious of the brevity of existence and the urgent need to put the turmoil of his life in order before meeting his Maker and his Judge. 'The business of life,' he wrote, 'is to work out our salvation; and the days are few, in which provision must be made for eternity.' Just how painful he found his pilgrimage is clear from his private prayers and meditations. For example, on Easter Eve 1761 he made his customary self-examination:

Since the Communion last Easter I have led a life so dissipated and useless, and my terrors and perplexities have so much increased, that I am under great depression and discouragement, yet I purpose to present myself before God tomorrow with humble hope that he will not break the bruised reed. Come unto me all ye that travail. I have resolved, I hope not presumptuously, till I am afraid to resolve again. Yet hoping in God, I steadfastly purpose to lead a new life. O God enable me, for Jesus Christ's sake.

He did not parade these thoughts before his friends. What they heard in his conversation – what they read in his published essays – were the measured, authoritative pronouncements of a 'majestic teacher of moral and religious wisdom'. What we can now see, with the evidence of his private journal before us, is the extent to which his public opinions, delivered with such force and certainty, were the product of doubt and anguish. His conclusions were thoroughly grounded in the harsh experience of living.

He recalled an early instance of his encounter with a hostile world. At the age of four he attended widow Oliver's school in

Lichfield. One day, the servant who accompanied him on the short journey to school failed to arrive to conduct him home. Young Samuel set off on his own. His schoolteacher, knowing how independent he liked to be, thought it best to follow him at a discreet distance. She noticed that as the sturdy little figure crossed the busy road, he stopped at the open drain which, as was then the custom, ran down the centre of the street. The child's eyesight was so bad that he had to get down on all fours, bringing his face to within inches of the stinking ditch and its foul contents before he could see sufficiently clearly to judge its width and jump across.

Close acquaintance with the ugly realities of life and the disfigurements of our nature gave him material for his reflections on human conduct. These he published in his twice weekly paper, *The Rambler.* Each essay, averaging 1,400 words in length, was hammered out against the printer's deadline, Tuesday and Saturday, over a period of two years. As with many gifted columnists, it was only extreme pressure that roused him from natural indolence. His essay on procrastination was 'hastily composed in Sir Joshua Reynolds's parlour, while the boy waited to carry it to the press'.

The self-imposed discipline of composing these moral essays was founded upon a deeply serious intention: to inculcate 'wisdom and piety' and 'the regulation of common life'. He prepared himself for the task by asking God's guidance in the words of a specially written prayer:

Almighty God, the giver of all good things, without whose help all labour is ineffectual, and without whose grace all wisdom is folly, grant, I beseech thee, that in this my undertaking thy Holy Spirit may not be withheld from me, but that I may promote thy glory, and the salvation both of myself and others...

It was Johnson's persistent belief in the possibility of our redemption through Jesus Christ which saved his writing from pessimism. There is, even in his bleakest passages, a tenderness towards his fellow beings, which gives his work a warmth and grandeur lacking in the writing of that other eighteenth century critic of the human condition, Jonathan Swift. In his essay on *Anger*, Johnson delineates with painful accuracy the character of the man who prides himself on having a short fuse:

> *There is in the world a certain class of mortals, known, and contentedly known, as passionate men, who imagine themselves entitled by that distinction to be provoked on every slight occasion, and to vent their rage in vehement and fierce vociferations...*

He concludes by moving his reader not to despise but to pity the man who, having consumed his life in anger, faces loneliness in old age:

> *When the vigour of youth fails him, and his amusements pall with frequent repetition, his occasional rage sinks by decay into peevishness... The world falls off from around him, and he is left to devour his own heart in solitude and contempt.*

> (Rambler no. 11)

To his generation which looked with heartless indifference upon the public spectacle of the gallows, Johnson had this to say:

> *On the days when the prisons of this city are emptied into the grave, let every spectator of the dreadful procession put the same question to his own heart ('who knows whether*

this man is not less culpable than me?'). Few among those
that crowd in thousands to the legal massacre, and look with
carelessness, perhaps triumph, on the utmost exacerbations of
human misery, would then be able to return without horror
and dejection. For who can congratulate himself upon a life
passed without some act more mischievous to the peace or
prosperity of others, than the theft of a piece of money?

(Rambler no. 114)

The irony of that final tinkling phrase – *the theft of a piece of
money* – following upon the massive thunder of the preceding
sentences tells us much about Johnson's rage against society's
guilty collusion in a corrupt law.

His flashes of anger were infrequent, and therefore
the more effective. In 1757 he was asked to review Soame
Jenyns's *A Free Enquiry into the Nature and Origin of Evil.* It was
a book which was enjoying some success, not least because it
peddled the popular doctrine of cosmic optimism first made
fashionable by Pope in his *Essay on Man* ('Whatever is, is right'),
and later lampooned by Voltaire in *Candide* ('All is for the best
in the best of all possible worlds'). The poor, wrote Jenyns,
are fortunate because they are exempt from the annoyances
which vex the rich. Ignorance is, 'A cordial administered by
the gracious hand of providence, of which [the poor] ought
never to be deprived by an ill-judged and improper education.'

*Yes, the poor are indeed insensible of many little vexations
which sometimes embitter the possessions and pollute
the enjoyments of the rich. They are not pained by casual
incivility or mortified by the mutilation of a compliment; but
this happiness is like that of a malefactor who ceases to feel
the cords that bind him when the pincers are tearing his flesh.*

The trouble with Pope and Jenyns, said Johnson, was that they had never seen poverty. In short they did not know what they were talking about. He did. That is what gave his utterances their authority.

Another scandal of his time was the incarceration of debtors at the pleasure of their creditors. Twenty thousand debtors, it had been calculated, languished in prison with no prospect of release. Of these a quarter perished yearly 'overborne by sorrow, consumed by famine, or putrified by filth; many of them in the most vigorous and useful part of their life'. He argued that the creditor himself should bear the blame, and called for a change of attitude until such time as 'universal infamy shall pursue [the creditor] whose wantonness of power, or revenge of disappointment, condemns another to torture and ruin; till he shall be hunted through the world as an enemy to man, and find riches no shelter from contempt'. (Idler no. 38)

To a woman who declared her abhorrence of drunkenness and could not understand 'what pleasure men can take in making beasts of themselves', he replied, 'I wonder, Madam, that you have not penetration enough to see the strong inducement to this excess; for he who makes a beast of himself gets rid of the pain of being a man.'

Johnson understood that inducement, though for long periods he abstained altogether. To a friend he admitted, 'I require wine, only when I am alone. I have then often wished for it, and often taken it.' 'What, by way of a companion, Sir?' 'To get rid of myself, to send myself away.'

What was his problem? Why did his faith bring him so little comfort? One reason may be found in his first lesson in religion, received from his mother as he sat with her in bed early one morning, aged three. She told him that we have two alternative destinations: heaven and hell. Our business in this life is to prepare ourselves for the final judgement which will determine to which of the two we shall go. The fact that the boy's mother was a niggler, and never left him in any doubt about his shortcomings, did nothing to comfort him. Throughout his life he never felt forgiven. It was only a few weeks before his death that the clouds parted at last and he came to know the assurance of God's love. As his friends came to take their leave, he spoke of God's grace at work in him: 'I have had such rays of hope shot into my soul, as have almost persuaded me that I am in a state of reconciliation with God.'

The other great influence was William Law's *Serious Call to a Devout and Holy Life*. He had read others – Hooker, Baxter, Taylor, for example, and the Church Fathers – but it was Law who convinced him of 'the necessity of a devout spirit, or habit of mind, in every part of our common life, in the discharge of all our business, in the use of all the gifts of God'. He had taken up Law's book, he told Boswell, 'expecting to find it a dull book (as such books generally are), and perhaps to laugh at it. But I found Law quite an overmatch for me; and this was the first occasion of my thinking in earnest of religion, after I became capable of rational enquiry'.

Johnson composed his last prayer a week before his death. By then he had asked his doctor to remove his drugs. 'I will take no more physic, not even my opiates: for I have prayed that I may render up my soul to God unclouded.' As his friends gathered at his bedside to join him in Holy Communion, they heard him pray:

> *Almighty and most merciful God, I am now, as to human eyes it seems, about to commemorate, for the last time, the death of thy Son Jesus Christ, our Saviour and Redeemer. Grant, O Lord, that my whole hope and confidence may be in his merits, and thy mercy; enforce and accept my imperfect repentance; make this available to the confirmation of my faith, the establishment of my hope, and the enlargement*

of my charity; and make the death of thy Son Jesus Christ effectual to my redemption. Have mercy upon me, and pardon the multitude of my offences. Bless my friends; have mercy upon all men. Support me, by thy Holy Spirit, in the days of weakness, and at the hour of death; receive me, at my death, to everlasting happiness, for the sake of Jesus Christ.

In his prayer he did not forget his friends. For him friendship was a precious gift. 'A man, Sir, should keep his friendship in constant repair,' he said, and no one strove more than him to follow this advice. It was the range of his friendships as well as their endurance which reveal the warmth and generosity of his nature. He crossed the conventional barriers of age, wealth, education, social status, success and taste. Although it is true that his London coterie included only those whose wit and conversation could match his, there were others of no conversation at all whose friendship he honoured as highly.

One of these was Harry Jackson, a failed cutler who had turned to drink. He was disparaged by Boswell as 'a low man, dull and untaught'. When Jackson died, Johnson wrote to Boswell, 'It was a loss, and a loss not to be repaired, as he was one of the companions of my childhood.'

And who could imagine two less likely companions than Johnson and Boswell? We have been given a telling glimpse of the older man's affection for his rackety young biographer. Boswell records how Johnson, thirty years his senior, insisted upon accompanying him to Harwich so that he could see him off on his journey to Holland. Johnson stood on the beach to wave goodbye. 'As the vessel put out to sea,' wrote Boswell, 'I kept my eyes upon him for a considerable time, while he remained rolling his majestic frame in his usual manner; and at last I perceived him walk back into the town and, and he disappeared.'

What Dr Johnson gave his wide circle of friends was convivial friendship and the benefit of clear thinking. 'He qualified our minds to think justly,' said one of them. But we must not think of him as the pompous pundit, for ever making pronouncements. His orotund diction was not without a touch of self-mockery. Besides, he did not always 'talk for victory'. He once said that 'the happiest conversation is that of which nothing is remembered but a general effect of pleasing impression'.

What he gave his readers was a large body of literary criticism and biography, the first English Dictionary, a novel, some poetry and a magnificent procession of moral essays. What he has left his church is the private record of a continuous religious struggle – an account of one of the outstanding pilgrimages of his generation.

Reading Dr Johnson now, two and a half centuries later, we are aware of the widening gap. Our ship sails on. The shore recedes. But looking back it is still possible to see that figure on the distant beach waving farewell at us across the years and 'rolling his magnificent frame'.

ST VALENTINE AND LORD HARDWICKE

(First published in the *Church Times*, February 2004,
to mark the two hundred and fiftieth anniversary of
the Hardwicke Marriage Act of 1754.)

Chaucer celebrates marriage in his poem about St Valentine's Day, *The Parlement of Foules*. He describes the Garden of Love where God's deputy, Nature, holds her court. She has summoned, as she does each year, all the birds of every kind to choose their mates. Before they do so, however, there is a long and noisy debate over the claims of three rival suitors to the female eagle. Everyone chips in. The cuckoo is cynical. The goose is mocked. The turtle dove is judicious; she speaks of constancy. The duck is blatant:

> *By my hat!*
> *That men should loven alway, causëless,*
> *Who can a reason find, or wit, in that?*
> *Daunceth he merry that is myrthëless?*

After more of this badinage, Nature intervenes and tells the young eagle that she must choose for herself. She panics and tells her suitors that she will have to think about it. They must come back next year for her answer. All the birds then sing a song (to a French tune, Chaucer tell us) and fly off with their chosen partners.

This poem is an allegory, written on the occasion of the marriage of Anne of Bohemia to King Richard II in 1382. Chaucer brings humour to a genre not known for levity. As a piece of court verse it is exceptional. What it says about love and marriage (and what it does not say) throws light upon contemporary attitudes to matrimony.

In his poem Chaucer takes us into a world ruled by God's chosen deputy, Nature, where people are free to wed according to their own devices, and matrimony is a private arrangement between consenting partners. That this garden of delight existed, even if only in people's minds, reflects the traditional view that marriage, in the words of the twentieth-century liturgist Bishop Walter Frere, is 'a natural compact, not a religious ceremony'.

Four hundred years after Chaucer wrote his *Parlement of Foules*, a different Parliament enacted Lord Hardwicke's Marriage Bill of 1753. Its full title was 'An Act for the better preventing of clandestine marriages'. It became effective on 25 March 1754, and was the first step towards our modern state-controlled institution of matrimony. During those intervening centuries the balance between marriage as a private contract on the one hand and, on the other, as a publicly regulated undertaking, tipped gradually towards the latter.

In the Middle Ages and during the early post-Reformation years it had been the church, not the state, which had sought to regulate marriage. The public declaration of banns, for example, had been made a requirement by the Synod of Westminster in 1200. The church had drawn up a table of prohibited degrees of kinship and affinity within which a marriage was void. However, what the clergy could not do was control the wide variety of folk customs by which their flock entered the married state. These differed from place to place, but usually involved a sequence of events over a period of weeks. The ceremony in the parish church (or, to be exact, at the church door) was only one of many in a chain of events, and it was the only one which needed the presence of a priest.

The process of marrying might start years earlier with an undertaking uttered by the two parties to each other before witnesses. If the words were spoken in the present tense and the proposed contract was neither bigamous nor within the prohibited degrees, it was a marriage. If the words were uttered in the future tense, it was not. In the latter case it was a pre-contract intention and was sometimes used between children below the marriageable age of fourteen (in the case of the boy) and twelve (in the case of the girl). In the event of the couple's subsequently engaging in sexual intercourse, even if still underage, the pre-contract intention was deemed by their act to have become contractually binding. Their voluntary bodily union confirmed their earlier verbal promise and so they were, by their own action, married. The records of matrimonial suits, usually arising from property and inheritance disputes, show that these irregular liaisons were recognised by the ecclesiastical courts as valid marriages.

From this it can be seen that what made the marriage was the consent declared by the couple to each other before witnesses. However desirable the church's blessing may have been in terms of pastoral discipline, according to canon law a religious ceremony was not necessary to effect or validate the union. Understandably the clergy often taught differently, but they did so against the teaching of their own canonists. Evidence suggests that the overwhelming majority of couples did in fact seek the church's blessing, albeit as confirmation of an existing union contracted earlier in private.

An example of the serial nature of marriage is provided by the case of William Whiteway, a citizen of Dorchester. In his diary, quoted in R B Outhwaite's *Clandestine Marriage in England 1500–1850* p xx (1995), he records:

April 6th 1620. Was concluded the marriage betwixt me Wm Whiteway and Eleanor Parkins, my best beloved wife which I pray God to bless and prosper.

May 4th 1620. The said W.W. and E.P. were bewrothed in my father Parkins his hall about 9 of the clock at night, by Mr John White in the presence of our parents, Uncle John Gould, C.Darby, and their wives, my cousin Joan Gould widow, and my sister Margarie Parkins.

June 14th 1620. I William Whiteway was married to Eleanor Parkins by Mr John White in the Church of Holy Trinity in Dorchester, in the presence of the greatest part of the town, which marriage I pray God to bless that it may turn to his glory and our good, and the comfort of all our friends.

William Whiteway was a God-fearing and respectable citizen. He was on good terms with the parson and involved him in the earlier stages of the marriage process. It was not always so. Many couples married without resort to the church.

As can be imagined, this state of affairs troubled the clergy. There were other forces, too, at work, more powerful than the church, which sought to regulate and institutionalise this 'natural compact'. Lawyers, striving to protect the interests of their clients, found it irksome that so many alleged marriages and consequent claims to inheritance depended upon the slender evidence of unregistered private contracts. The aristocracy and the landed gentry, concerned to protect their property and their families' reputations, were alarmed that their teenage daughters could so easily fall victim to unscrupulous suitors in search of a rich settlement.

For almost a century Parliament debated and rejected a succession of measures to meet this problem. By the mid-eighteenth century another factor was at work. Rogue clergy had found a source of income in officiating at irregular marriages, sometimes in private houses, sometimes in taverns, sometimes in churches. A particularly notorious centre of this trade was the Fleet prison for debtors. Among the inmates were usually to be found a number of clerics, who were willing to sell their services in the neighbouring taverns.

Hardwicke's Marriage Act of 1753 sought to put a stop to these scandals. Severe penalties were introduced. For performing a marriage without banns or licence a clergyman faced fourteen years' transportation to His Majesty's plantations in America. For a false entry in the newly-introduced marriage register he could be hanged. From 26 March 1754 all marriages in England and Wales had to be conducted by an ordained minister of the Church of England, according to the Book of Common Prayer, in a licensed church and between the canonical hours of eight in the morning and midday. Any marriage which did not conform to these rules was declared not only irregular, but null and void, as were those granted by licence to minors without parental consent. Marriage was now a monopoly conferred by parliament upon the Church of England. Only Jews, Quakers and royalty were exempt from the Act.

By this Act the state had adopted much that was already contained in canon law, but by enacting these measures as statute law enforceable in the secular courts, and by asserting an authority which the church had never claimed – that of declaring void those contracts hitherto regarded as valid but irregular – it had established matrimony as a state-controlled institution. And it had bound the church to itself as the instrument by which its will would be done.

Some of the bishops were uneasy. They felt that the state was taking to itself powers which it had no right to possess, but they were reluctant to oppose a bill whose purpose was to clear up some of the most flagrant scandals of the age. It was left to Henry Fox, amongst others, to object in the Commons that in setting aside all irregular marriages the bill was 'making free with the laws of God and nature'.

Much of the Hardwicke Act was repealed by later legislation. The 1836 Act opened the way to civil marriages and permitted Roman Catholics and other nonconformists to conduct weddings in their own churches. However, what remains of the 1753 Act is the basic principle that in law it is the state which determines the manner in which the marital status is defined and conferred. This attempt to control by legislation an aspect of human conduct so richly varied and anarchic as love has never really worked. Co-habitation, either as a preliminary to a public wedding or not, is not new, and need not be evidence of promiscuity.

When it came to choosing partners, Chaucer ascribed the presiding influence to the 'goddess Nature'. In matters matrimonial it was she, not the church (and certainly not the state), who was God's deputy. He had a good precedent. Jesus, in his debate with the Pharisees, appealed to a higher authority than the Mosaic Law. Marriage, he said, was to be understood not within the terms of rabbinic tradition, but in the wider context of Creation and the laws of nature as described in the story of Adam and Eve.

JAMES WOODFORDE

1740–1803
Country Parson and Diarist

(First published in the *Church Times*, January 2003.)

Parson Woodforde twice had occasion to take offence at someone's hat. As an undergraduate at Oxford he observed in his diary that 'Mercer (who wore a gold laced hat) was very drunk and very abusive'. There had been an unseemly fracas in New College garden one afternoon in May 1763, when Woodforde and some friends had been joined by unwelcome intruders and he was left to pay the bill for the broken wine glasses. 'Mr Mercer behaved very unlike a gentleman,' he complained, and one gets the impression that, apart from the drunken abuse, it was the man's hat which riled the diarist.

Many years later Woodforde, by now a middle-aged country parson of ample glebe and settled opinions, was enraged by another hat. This time it was the 'frenchyfied... *chapeau de brache* [sic]' carried by Mr Jeans at a dinner party. The *chapeau-bras* in question was a folded silk accessory designed to be held under the arm at court. Its owner on this occasion was the incumbent of a neighbouring parish, and he and Woodforde were guests of the Townshends of Honingham Hall. Also present at the dinner was Mrs Cornwallis, the widow of the former Archbishop of Canterbury. Whereas Woodforde knew how to behave in the presence of his social superiors Jeans, it appears, did not. He was a social climber and an embarrassment. His affected talk, his debts, his extravagant mismanagement of his parsonage, his long absences from his parish – and his hat – were all of a piece. How different, how very different he was from the circumspect Mr Woodforde.

James Woodforde was a dullish fellow, but unlike the rackety Mr Jeans he kept his hand to the plough, first in Somerset for ten years as a country curate, then for three years at New College, Oxford, as Fellow and sub-warden, and finally for the remaining twenty-seven years of his life as Rector of Weston Longville in Norfolk. He was a conscientious pastor and preacher, but it is by his diary that he is remembered.

His reputation has suffered from the popularity of his edited diary, first published in the 1920s, and still in print. The great length of the original needed selection; the selection needed an angle; the book needed to sell. As a result Parson Woodforde is more widely known for his dinners than his devotion. It is a distortion which the Parson Woodforde Society, through its publications, has done much to correct, in particular through Roy Winstanley's *Parson Woodforde: The Life and Times of a Country Diarist.**

Why should we read the journal of an eighteenth-century country priest, in whose life there was no blemish of scandal, no disturbance of doubt, no agitation of zeal and no greater stir of emotion than a passing irritation caused by someone's hat? Why, indeed, if not for his dinners?

But there was more to the parson than jugged hare.

James Woodforde lived in that long Georgian afternoon before the rise of Bonaparte. In his diary we hear and see and almost smell an England which vanished at the coming of the railway. It was not a golden age. In many ways it was cruel, corrupt and ugly. It was a land both recognisable and yet wholly alien from ours. The parsonage, where he was born in 1740, still stands today, as do the churches he served in

---

* www.parsonwoodforde.org.uk

Somerset and Norfolk. Winchester and New College, where he was educated, have hardly altered in appearance.

The lanes he rode along as curate of Castle Cary and the road he travelled between Weston Longville and Norwich are still the same, but when he knew them they were part of the countryside they traversed. They had not yet become the urban corridors we know today.

Many of the field boundaries remain; even their names are remembered and used. With so many of the landmarks he knew still visible, it is not possible to read his words without a start of recognition. The similarity, however, conceals how foreign from ours was the land he knew.

Take, for example, the subject usually associated with Woodforde: food. The following is a typical extract:

> *Mr Howes and Wife and Mrs Davy, Mr Bodham and his Brother, and Mr du Quesne all dined and spent the afternoon and part of the evening with us to-day. I gave them for dinner a dish of Maccarel, three young Chicken boiled and some Bacon, a neck of Pork rosted and a Gooseberry Pye hot. We laughed immoderately after dinner on Mrs Howes's being sent to Coventry by us for an hour. What with laughing and eating hot Gooseberry Pye brought on me the Hickupps with a violent pain in my stomach which lasted till I went to bed. At Cards Quadrille this evening – lost 0. 2. 6.*

We do not know how this meal was eaten. How large were the helpings? Did his guests pick and choose, or did they devour everything that was set before them? Woodforde does not tell us. We know that most of the men, and some of the women, would have spent much of the day out of doors walking and riding. Even carriage exercise on rutted un-metalled lanes was physically demanding. Woodforde and his guests needed protein.

However, the real difference between his food and ours is not the quantity, but its production and preparation. In the days before the commercialisation of food, people lived alongside the beasts and fowls and crops they ate. Woodforde farmed forty-six acres of glebe. Much of the food that appeared on his dinner table, with the exception on this occasion of the mackerel, had been reared and nurtured on the land outside his window. He, his niece, Nancy, who lived with him, his 'farming man' Ben Leggett, his manservant Will Coleman, the cook, the maid and the boy, would all have been directly involved in the process of food production and preparation.

The menu for the daily dinner was, therefore, not merely a gratuitous catalogue of prepared meats and pastries, the product of other people's work and described with the offensive relish of a modern food critic. It was the culmination of a household's chief industry and purpose, which was the sustenance and survival of its members.

This physical intimacy with the land and the weather – with the reality of cold and damp, heat and drought, sunshine and darkness, surfeit and hunger – gives Woodforde's diary a particular significance for our dislocated society. When an Englishman lived only one failed harvest away from famine, he said his Grace with feeling.

The continuity of field and food, of master and servant, of market town and countryside, was part of a greater continuity. In the eighteenth century it was still possible to think of church and state as two sides of one coin. Religion had not retreated into its corner. In that mild climate of religious opinion, churchgoing and Christian belief were nothing remarkable, and a man's ordination to the priesthood was not considered an interruption or deviation from the social obligations of his class, but a continuation of the same.

Parson Woodforde and his contemporaries have been pilloried by later generations for their lack of religious ardour.

Theirs seems to us to have been a very worldly sort of faith. And it is true that Woodforde's references to his clerical duties are perfunctory. 'I read prayers and preached this morning at Weston' is usually the most he gives us. We should not be surprised. The performance of his weekly task called for little comment in a world which took such things for granted. Our mistake is to think that because it was a routine function it was done without sincerity.

His sermons, fifty-nine of which survive, give a better measure of his religion than his diary. As was usual in those days Woodforde copied and adapted his material from the printed sermons of others – amongst them John Tillotson, Francis Atterbury and Richard Sterne. Even so, his selection and rewriting reveals his own belief and practice. In his preaching he instructs his congregation not only to lead moral and sober lives, but to be regular and sincere in their private prayers, to attend public worship and to receive the sacrament of Holy Communion with great care and devotion, for by it 'a conveyance is made of all the benefits of Christ's sacrifice on the Cross'.

He was a conscientious visitor of the sick and dying. Typical is his entry for 9 June 1787: 'I went and read Prayers again this morning to Mrs Leggatt and administered also the Holy Sacrament to her – she was very weak and but just alive. She was sensible and showed marks of great satisfaction after receiving... Pray God bless her.'

References to his clerical duties, however, are far outnumbered by those to the incidents and preoccupations of daily life. He never married. For most of his life at Weston his niece, Nancy, acted as his housekeeper. The vagaries of her health are the subject of frequent comment: 'Nancy complained very much this morning of the Wind in her Stomach – I desired her to drink Beer after Dinner instead of wine, which she did and was better after it.' On other occasions he recommended rhubarb, of which over the years she consumed large quantities. More alarmingly Mr Thorne, the local physician, prescribed port: 'more rather than less'. Woodforde records, 'She drank to day between a Pint and a Quart without having the least effect upon the Brain. She has not drank [*sic*] less than a Pint for many Days. Dinner today, Tripe boiled and cold Beef etc.'

Domestic tiffs are recorded, but not in great detail. 'Nancy was pert to day' is the usual indication that they had quarrelled. Sometimes Nancy was *saucy* – a term of great opprobrium in Woodforde's vocabulary. Seldom was the peace of the household so severely shattered as when one evening his manservant Will Coleman, who for long had nursed an unrequited passion for Lizzie, the housemaid, went off his head, attacked the cook, ran from the house and jumped into the pond.

He records the round of social visits and dinners. At the top of his list of engagements are his invitations to Weston House, the home of Squire Custance and his lady. There grew up between parson and squire a friendship almost uninhibited, but not entirely, by the difference in their social standing.

More relaxed were the dinners he shared with his friends among the local clergy. They had formed a dining club – or 'rotation' – which met by turns in each other's homes. It was at one of these, when Woodforde was host, that four clergy and their wives and children, were invited to dinner. They stayed for supper and spent the night. It was one of the few occasions when the rather solemn parson threw decorum to the winds. He and two of the clergy sat up all night playing cards and were 'exceeding merry'. 'At six in the morning,' he wrote, 'we serenaded the folks that were a-bed with our best on the hautboy.'

His relationship to the local farmers was cordial and business-like. They were obliged to pay him tithes, from which he drew most of his income. In those days an incumbent was in direct, and sometimes uncomfortable, contact with the sources of his stipend. Here was another continuity.

To encourage punctual payment, Woodforde invited the tithe payers every December to an annual audit. This was followed by what he called a 'frolic', or dinner. In 1795 twenty-three farmers sat down to 'a Rump of Beef, a slip-marrow bone of Beef, both boiled, a Leg of Mutton boiled and Capers, a fine Surloin of Beef, Salt Fish, a Couple of Rabbits boiled and Onion Sauce, and plumb and plain puddings in plenty. Small Beer and strong, Punch and Wine as much as they pleased to make use of. Strong Beer amazingly liked and drank in great Quantity, six Bottles of Rum made into Punch, one Dozen of Lemons, and about five Bottles of Port Wine drank today. They were all extremely well pleased with their entertainment and very harmonious.' The last of his guests did not leave until 2am Woodforde collected a little short of £287, a considerable sum in those days.

His recreations and his attitudes were those of an eighteenth-century country gentleman. With his greyhounds he coursed hares and rabbits for his table. He fished the local rivers. From time to time he rode into Norwich, or went in his carriage with Nancy, to visit the shops and the theatre. He marvelled at Mr Decker's ascent in a hot air balloon from Quantrells Gardens. He smoked a pipe, took snuff and drank in moderation. He received occasional deliveries of smuggled liquor and tobacco, left at night on his doorstep by the local blacksmith.

He observed the harsh exaction of the law without sentiment, but not without a sense of justice. When he rode out to Baddeley Moor to view the corpse of a murderer hanging in chains, he remarked how deeply mired the ground had become by the traffic of sightseers. He witnessed a thief being whipped through the streets of Castle Cary, but refused to contribute to the collection made for the public hangman who carried out the punishment. He was a supporter of the House of Hanover and fired a cannon on his lawn to mark the king's birthday. He worried about the steep rise in prices and his loss in real income, but declined to exact higher tithes from his parishioners.

When he became too ill to perform his parish duties, he paid others to do so. Incumbents did not retire; there was no need to and, besides, there were no pensions. Like his father before him, he died in his parsonage, observing to the end the continuity of life and work. The last entry in his diary, made only hours before he suffered the stroke which killed him, ends with the words, 'Dinner today, Roste Beef etc.'

ATHELSTAN RILEY

1858–1945
Anglo-Catholic Churchman, Traveller,
Hymn-Writer and Author

(First published in *The World of Church Music 1986.*)

When Athelstan Riley's mother asked the dame of his private
school how he was getting on, she was told, 'Teaching that
boy Riley, Ma'am, is like dragging out your guts with a fish
hook!' – an early tribute to the combative qualities of this
most energetic churchman, traveller and Anglo-Catholic
campaigner. Although few people now will know more
about him than his authorship of the hymn 'Ye watchers and
ye holy ones', during his lifetime (1858–1945) there could
have been fewer who had not at one time or another been
cheered or irritated by his frequent and trenchant incursions
into ecclesiastical debate. Outstanding in his long career was
his pioneering work for Anglican-Orthodox relations and his
joint editorship of the *English Hymnal* (1906), both of which
have greatly enriched contemporary Anglicanism.

Possessed of a considerable fortune inherited from his
father and of a faith which he claimed owed much to the
influence of his governess, who was an ardent Tractarian,
and to that of his mother's lady's maid, who was a devout
evangelical, Athelstan Riley devoted much of his energies
and a considerable part of his wealth to the service of the
Church of England and to the vindication of its Catholic
tradition. He was one of a handful of wealthy Victorian
laypeople who used their leisure and talent to the great

advantage of the High Church movement in the post-Tractarian period.

One of the first people to be influenced by his enthusiasm for the Catholic revival was his schoolfriend W J Birkbeck, who was later to become the leading authority on the Russian Church and not least of whose achievements was to introduce into Anglican worship the Russian Contakion for the Dead. This was sung at the request of Queen Victoria at the memorial services of Tsar Alexander III and her grandson, the Duke of Clarence. It was later included in the English Hymnal.

At Eton Riley and Birkbeck used to supplement the thin liturgical diet provided in the college chapel by slipping away to worship at St Stephen's, Clewer. When they and some other boys petitioned the headmaster for an early celebration of Holy Communion once a month in addition to the monthly late celebration he was shocked by the suggestion, and told them, 'I cannot encourage superstition.'

After leaving Pembroke College, Oxford, where he revived the archaic status of *sophister*, which entitled an undergraduate who had passed 'Responsions' to wear a black hood with his gown, he went to Cuddesdon College to train for the priesthood. Later, he gave up his intention to be ordained, but not before he had preached his College Sermon, which was on obedience. This was an interesting subject to be chosen by one who was to spend so much energy attacking 'latitudinising' bishops. It is ironic that as an exemplar of obedience he cited in his sermon Mary, ascribing to her the title *Theotokos* (God-bearer) which was later to bring down so much episcopal wrath upon his use of it in his hymn 'Ye watchers and ye holy ones'.

In 1883, at the age of twenty-four, he set out in the company of a young priest, Arthur Owen, to explore Mount Athos. Although the railway had greatly improved the safety and comfort of travel, and although Constantinople was now within five days of Paris, an expedition through territories of the Ottoman Empire was still a hazardous undertaking for two young Englishmen without a word of Turkish between them. However, Riley was a resourceful traveller. He carried with him a gun, an India-rubber sponge bag and a *lévinge*. 'My bath goes into the compass of a large sponge bag, and does not take up more room in the portmanteau than an ordinary nightshirt. It has been many thousand miles with me and is in as good condition as when I first bought it for seventeen shillings and sixpence.' The *lévinge* was a sleeping bag, consisting of a cane hoop and a double compartment of calico muslin, ingeniously designed to repel bugs. It was an essential part of an Englishman's luggage when visiting Turkish inns and Greek monasteries.

Riley's account, published in 1887, of his three months on Mount Athos not only gives a valuable and detailed description of the condition and customs of monasteries, but, by introducing to the English public a Christian tradition hitherto so little known in the West, stimulated an interest in the Orthodox tradition which was to help remedy the rigid insularity of the Anglican church. At the time, however, it must have come as an unwelcome surprise to his readers to whom the words of the 'Ancient and Modern' hymn, 'Christian, dost thou see them' were so familiar, to be told that the skull of its seventh-century author, St Andrew of Crete, was still venerated as a sacred relic in the monastery of Vatopedi.

Riley's knowledge of the Levant persuaded Archbishop Benson to send him the following year to Kurdistan on a mission of enquiry into the state of the Assyrian (Nestorian) Church. The pathetic remnant of this once-great church had appealed in 1837 to the English Church for help, and again in 1876. 'We are like sheep without a shepherd... send us some of your missionaries and preachers to guide us in the way of life, for verily we have all gone astray.' Anglican clergy had been sent on both occasions. However, when Riley's small expeditionary party reached its destination, having trekked by mule through territory infested by brigands armed with flintlock muskets, they found the patriarch Mar Shimoun and his tiny flock reduced to the lowest level of ignorance and poverty. Only one of their number, the hermit Rabban Yonan, was able to read their sacred texts, and in his uncertain hands rested the sole custody of one of Christendom's most ancient liturgical texts, the rite of Addai and Mari. It was as a result of Riley's report that Archbishop Benson established the Assyrian Mission to rescue from extinction the beleaguered survivors of the pre-Chalcedonian Church.

Riley's membership of the London School Board, and his vigorous campaign in support of religious education during the 1890s, seem far removed from his work in the Middle East. He would, however, have seen no difference between a crusade to deliver the Assyrian Church from the rapacity of the Turk and a quest to protect English schoolchildren from the secularism of the state. He fought a series of battles to guarantee the place of religious education in the syllabus of the local authority schools. In these he found himself allied with Cardinal Vaughan, Archbishop of Westminster, who feared the growing secularism of the state – what Lord Halifax referred to as 'the sham of non-denominationalism'. 'The School Board Dragon,' wrote Riley to Halifax, 'will be forced to bow his head to the Virgin's Son.' The defeat in Parliament of the 1908 Education Bill, which contained proposals severely limiting religious education, was chiefly due to the energetic campaign led by Halifax and Riley outside Westminster.

His most enduring achievement was his co-editorship of the *English Hymnal*. In 1903 Percy Dearmer and Athelstan Riley gathered a small committee with the original intention of compiling a supplement to the *Hymns Ancient and Modern*. This compilation was eventually published in 1906 as the

English Hymnal, much of the work having be done at Riley's home in Kensington. Ralph Vaughan Williams, who had been persuaded by Dearmer to take on the musical editorship, later paid tribute to Riley's extensive knowledge of church music, and told how he would often come to his house to go through proofs or to suggest new tunes. Riley would arrive at Vaughan Williams' house in Barton Street, Westminster, 'on a white horse which he deputed a young relative of mine, a boy of about ten, to hold while he discussed hymns with me'.

Riley contributed three of his own hymns and nine translations from the Latin. Probably his best-known hymn is 'Ye Watchers and ye Holy Ones'. It was written at the request of Vaughan Williams who wished to include the fine German tune 'Lasst uns erfreuen' but could not find any words to fit. Riley's words include as the second verse a paraphrase of the Greek *Theotokon* (God Bearer), an ancient hymn to Mary, Mother of God, thereby introducing into the piety of the English Church a devotion which had been extinguished by Protestant scruple and was still, in 1906, strongly disapproved of by episcopal authority.

It is hard now to imagine the bitter opposition by many bishops to the *English Hymnal* when it first appeared. Gore tried to ban its use in the Diocese of Birmingham, as did G F Browne in Bristol, on the grounds that it encouraged invocation of the saints and that some of its Communion hymns expressed a Romish doctrine of the Eucharist. That the row subsided and the new book won a place in the church's worship was, in part, due to its obvious musical and literary merits, but also in part to Riley's vigorous propaganda. He gave numerous public lectures on the development of hymnody, illustrated by examples from the new book and assisted by a choir. These lectures were later published in the *Treasury* magazine, and subsequently in his book *Concerning Hymn Tunes and Sequences* (Mowbray, 1915), which is a highly readable combination

of musical scholarship and personal prejudice. An example
is provided by his views on the 'appalling *St Clement*' a tune
relegated to the appendix, or 'Chamber of Horrors', as Vaughan
Williams called it. 'A really bad tune,' wrote Riley. 'Note among
its faults the initial interval of a major sixth which compels a
portamento and thus, at the very beginning of the tune, induces
that ultra-sentimentality which is so characteristic of it. Again,
this interval coming before B and C accentuated the semi-
tonal interval which helps to give the tune its effeminacy.'

But Riley and his co-editors knew that they had to make
concessions to popular taste. However much they would have
preferred us to sing 'The day thou gavest, Lord, is ended' to
'Les Commandements de Dieu', the dignified tune from the
Genevan Psalter, they recognised the powerful appeal of a
barrel-organ melody like 'St Clement'. 'The *English Hymnal*
with all its scholarship and musical excellence,' wrote Riley,
'contains at least fifty tunes, and in my judgement more than
one hundred hymns, which are unworthy of the rest, but
which must be included if it is seriously intended to provide
for the necessities of the day.'

There were very few ecclesiastical issues which did not
engage Riley's active interest. Divorce Law reform, Prayer
Book revision, religious education, revival of the religious
communities, church ritual (he was for many years vice-
president of the Alcluin Club and of the Church Union) and
ecumenism (he was a delegate at the Lausanne Conference)
were some of the many topics which drew lively comment
from his pen. But his greatest joy was to travel, and he never
lost his zest for the discomforts and the beauty of the Levant,
an enthusiasm not shared by his young bride, Andalusia,
who after a particularly arduous journey in a horse-drawn
Turkish carriage, shocked her husband by declaring that the
grand mosque of Adrianople looked like a gasometer and that
the 'chimneys' of the smaller mosques put her in mind of

Sheffield.* Thereafter he usually travelled without her, going abroad every year and bringing back from the Orient amongst other souvenirs a taste for Turkish yoghurt, at a time when it was yet unknown in this country, and a penchant for Cypriot cigarettes.

His final skirmish took place in extreme old age. Refusing in 1940 at the age of eighty-two to return to England, he remained in his Jersey home, Trinity Manor, a property which gave him the title *Seigneur de la Trinité*. After the house had been requisitioned by the German army, he and his butler lived in the lodge. The Commandant, wishing to be kind to the old gentleman, sent word inviting him to visit his home whenever he wished. Riley's response was in character. He not only declined the invitation, but whenever he went for his afternoon walk he made a point of turning his back upon the house lest he should be reminded of its temporary and unwelcome guests. By the time Jersey was liberated he was in a nursing home, almost too ill to know that the combat to which he had contributed his own private gesture of defiance had been concluded in victory. He died on 17 November 1945. His body was buried in Jersey in Holy Trinity churchyard, but his heart was interred beside his wife in her chantry chapel in the Cornish Church of St Petroc Minor.

---

* For Andalusia Riley's travel journal see Jo Park, *Patron of St Petroc Minor*, Truro, 1982.

DOROTHY L SAYERS

1893–1957
Author, Scholar and Playwright

(First published in the *Church Times* to mark the
fiftieth anniversary of her death on 17 December 2007.)

The first thing that struck you about Dorothy L Sayers was her size. It was not something that worried her. 'The elephant is crated,' she gasped as, after a struggle, she subsided into the back of a friend's car. At Marshall and Snelgrove it took nine months to construct a corset robust enough to contain her.

Not that any conventional constraints ever restricted her for long. During a successful run of one of her plays in the West End she could be seen – and heard – entertaining the cast to large, bibulous suppers at the Soho restaurant, *Le Moulin d'Or*. Whole-hearted enjoyment characterised her approach not only to food and wine. When she lectured on Dante to the Society of Italian Studies at Cambridge, some of the academics were shocked by the vigour and élan of her delivery.

'Being no academic but a common popular soap-box lecturer, I didn't mind shouting at them in a loud and brassy voice without regard for my own dignity or that of my subject,' she told a friend. It was not only that she made sure that she could be heard (the other speakers had been inaudible), but that she spoke with passion. One of her audience, a young lecturer, Barbara Reynolds, wrote later to her: 'I got so excited that I had to be held down.'

The passion with which she lectured and wrote about the *Divine Comedy* encouraged others to read it as a contemporary work rather than a classic. She passed on what she herself had learnt from her friend and mentor, the author Charles Williams: to find its meaning 'in their own lives and love affairs'. There may have been better translations since hers, but her introductions in the Penguin Classics volumes of Dante's trilogy remain the best. It has been estimated that during the last half of the twentieth century they reached over one and a quarter million readers.

What so gripped her was the grandeur of Dante's vision, in which all human experience is integrated and judged by God's redemptive love – the contingencies of individual lives set in the grand design of salvation. What had triggered this insight in the poet's mind was the intense experience of his love for a Florentine girl – 'that first staggering shock of young love', as Williams put it.

Dorothy came to her knowledge of Dante in middle age. What she found in the *Divine Comedy* was a unity which appealed to her deepest desires. Hers was a passionately intellectual nature. In 1944 she wrote to Charles Williams that the present age had 'not only divorced the passions from the intellect, but has set them at enmity'.

In a passage from her semi-autobiographical (and incomplete) *Cat o' Mary*, we get another glimpse of what she was searching for. She attributes to her fictional self, Katherine Lammas, her own experience – one might call it a spiritual revelation – on the tennis court at her father's rectory at Bluntisham. After a wet spring the grass had grown over the metal plates which marked the corners of the court. The time had come to prepare the court for summer. Whilst her parents prodded the ground in a haphazard way, Katherine/Dorothy employed the Euclidean method of intersecting arcs to find the corners. She was following the theory she had learnt but never seen in practice. With peg and string she found the concealed corner plates. 'She had been brought face to face with beauty,' she wrote. 'It had risen up before her… the lovely unity of things: the wedding of the thing learned and the thing done: the great intellectual fulfilment… Nothing would ever quite wipe out the memory of that magnificent moment when the intersecting circles marched out of the pages of the Euclid book and met on the green grass in the sun-flecked shadow of the mulberry tree.'

Dorothy found 'the lovely unity of things' and the 'great intellectual fulfilment' in the great sweep of the church's history and doctrine. But hers was a gradual religious development. In *Cat o' Mary* Katherine's upbringing at the rectory reflects her own. Katherine's father 'actuated by God knows what sense of personal inadequacy, or nervous dread of intimate personal contact, sedulously refrained from giving any religious instruction to his daughter, beyond what she might pick up from regular weekly attendance at Morning and Evening Prayer'.

What religion she encountered at her boarding school was, if anything, even less helpful. She found the 'dreary pietism' and the emphasis upon 'feeling' quite off-putting. Years later, in a letter about her own son's religious instruction she wrote, 'The cultivation of religious emotion, without philosophic basis is thoroughly pernicious, in my opinion.' At Oxford an earnest cousin tried to interest her in the Christian Union. Dorothy replied, 'Certainly not! Speaking as a baptised and more or less educated member of the Catholic Church of Christ as in England by law established, certainly not!'

She attributed her deepening awareness of Christianity to G K Chesterton's *Orthodoxy*, which she had first read at school. If it had not been for that, she said, she might have given Christianity up altogether. She had been forcibly struck by his image of Christendom as a heavenly chariot 'thundering through the ages, the dull heresies sprawling and prostrate, the wild truth reeling but erect'.

She embraced the idea of Christian redemption with intellectual passion. In this she stood in the classical tradition of Christian spirituality, which admits no separation between heart and mind. Later, when she had become a recognised apologist for the Christian faith, she wrote, 'Of course, the experience of the presence of God is not the same as having opinions about Him. But false opinions are an obstacle to spiritual experience, and it is our business to remove those false opinions and cure that ignorance as far as we can.'

However, her work as a defender of the faith had to wait. She had to make a living. After coming down from Oxford with a First – where, according to Vera Brittain in *Testament of Youth*, she had been 'a bouncing and exuberant young female who always seemed to be preparing for tea-parties' – she took up, briefly, a post at Hull High School for Girls, then worked for a short while for the publisher and bookseller Basil Blackwell before working for a few months at a school in France. She eventually settled in Bloomsbury and in 1922 got a job with an advertising agency, where she remained until 1931.

From childhood Dorothy had always written, at first mostly verse. When she moved to Bloomsbury in 1920 she had hopes of surviving on her writing. The hopes were not fulfilled, and for a time it was, in her words, 'either food or curtains'. In desperation she wrote a novel: 'I've written a silly book, but I don't suppose any publisher will take it.' It was a detective story. The central character was the brilliant young aristocrat, Lord Peter Wimsey. 'He might go some way to providing bread and cheese,' she wrote.

She wanted to call her first Peter Wimsey novel *The Singular Adventures of the Man with the Golden Pince-Nez*. Her publishers had different ideas. *Whose Body?* when it appeared was a success. In the words of J I M Stewart (who wrote detective fiction under the pseudonym 'Michael Innes'), Lord Peter 'was equipped with learned and artistic interests, nonchalant manners, an insatiable interest in crime, and a reliable manservant named Bunter'. He also possessed 'a penetrating intelligence and outstanding powers of logical inference'. In writing for an educated readership whose members might secretly fancy they recognised in themselves characteristics similar to Lord Peter's, Dorothy had discovered a flattering and winning formula. There were twelve novels in all, the last (*Gaudy Night*) appearing in 1935.

Lord Peter had provided sufficient bread and cheese to enable Dorothy to leave her job at the advertising agency and to support herself for the rest of her life upon her literary earnings. This new freedom enabled her to turn to what she now regarded as her real work. As J I M Stewart said, perhaps a shade ruefully, 'The death of the detective was the birth of the Christian apologist.' Plays, articles, lectures, correspondence followed in a rich and steady flow until her death twenty-two years later in 1957. In 1937 she was commissioned to write a play for Canterbury Cathedral. *The Zeal of thy House* followed T S Eliot's *Murder in the Cathedral* (1935) and Charles Williams's *Thomas Cranmer of Canterbury* (1936). From December 1941 to October 1942 the BBC broadcast in monthly episodes her serial play *The Man Born to Be King*. It broke new ground in giving Jesus non-biblical words to speak. Not everyone was pleased.

During the 1940s her voice was heard speaking with growing authority on theological, literary and social issues. She was regarded, alongside C S Lewis, Charles Williams and T S Eliot, as a leading lay apologist for the Christian faith. Archbishop William Temple offered her a Lambeth DD. In a long letter explaining her reasons, she declined lest such an honour inhibit her freedom to speak her mind. 'I think I do fully understand... If I were in your position I should have reached your conclusion,' he replied.

'What a woman!' wrote Rosamund Essex in the *Church Times* (2 March 1979). 'Brilliant, erratic, rude and impatient as only dedicated writers and artists can be, earnest, hard-working, loving, yet never achieving settled love, deeply religious, with a flair for expressing old truths in new words, funny as well as witty, eccentric, curious in appearance, scholarly, a woman who knew her own mind and knew, too, that it was as good as any man's; a fighter who could be a worthy opponent in any kind of controversy.'

What a woman!

HOLLYWOOD AND GOD

(Written in 2003 to mark the fiftieth anniversary
of *The Robe*, the first film in CinemaScope)

Religion portrayed on the big screen can have unpredictable effects. Someone I know was so moved by a film about St Bernadette that she was asked to leave the cinema. In the foyer she was helped by a kindly usherette to a seat, where she sobbed and sobbed with laughter.

It is not the fault of Hollywood that our response to solemnity can sometimes be so wildly inappropriate. Charles Lamb confessed that 'anything awful' made him laugh. 'I was at Hazlitt's marriage, and had like to have been turned out several times during the ceremony,' he wrote, adding, 'I misbehaved once at a funeral.'

But it is not only our nervousness when confronted by the hushed tones of piety that makes us giggle. There are other reasons why Hollywood's biblical epics provided such a feast of fun. As a genre they were always spectacular. In 1912 the earliest version of *Quo Vadis* gave audiences their first flickering glimpses of Roman decadence and Christian martyrdom. Recognising the box-office potential of religion, Cecil B DeMille decided to try his hand. His first attempt, a film about St Joan, called *The Woman Joan*, failed. It was gloomy, there was no 'love interest', and medieval Rouen was no substitute for Nero's Rome.

DeMille went down-market. He began to make saucy comedies, with titles like *New Wives for Old*, in which a recurring feature was the bath scene. Profoundly respectable American audiences liked to be mildly shocked, so long as virtue triumphed during the last reel. After succeeding with comedies, DeMille decided to return to the biblical epic, bringing to it the lesson he had learnt: that people like to be assured that sin is wrong, but only after they have been shown that it can also be fun.

His first version of *The Ten Commandments* (1923) was a huge success. He introduced a non-biblical sub-plot and a modern morality tale (in his remake of 1956 he dropped the latter). The storyline was a gift for the special effects department. The burning bush, the seven plagues of Egypt, the parting of the Red Sea, the drowning of Pharaoh's host, the golden calf and the wrath of God were translated to the screen with magnificent bravura.

In *The Sign of the Cross* (1932) – a 'talkie' – Claudette Colbert, as the Empress Poppaea, appeared in, and out of, her bath. Charles Laughton, as Nero, was debauched and mad. Slaves abounded, senators conspired in the steam bath, eunuchs eavesdropped behind pillars, gladiators fought and died horribly in the arena, and Christians were fed to the lions. By now the formula had been set for the next forty years.

Many of the elements of imperial Rome were transferred to the Middle East – the crowds of extras, the heat, the sandals and, with a little adjustment, most of the costumes. Although the architecture of ancient Israel or New Testament Palestine gave Hollywood less scope than Rome, the film designers made the most of their opportunities. Solomon's palace, the court of King Ahasuerus, Belshazzar's banqueting hall and Pontius Pilate's praetorium gave them licence to build lavish sets depicting marble halls, stairways, fountains and colonnades.

Nor were feasting and debauchery the exclusive prerogative of first-century Rome. Nineveh, Babylon, Gaza, Herod's court in Jerusalem, the cities of the plain and the riot of misbehaviour that broke out amongst the Israelites as they capered round the Golden Calf in the Wilderness of Sinai – all offered immense cinematic opportunities.

The deployment of thousands of extras – twelve thousand people and fifteen thousand animals in the 1956 *Ten Commandments* – in a series of vast *tableaux vivants* was an extension of the nineteenth-century tradition. Artists of the Victorian era like William Etty and John Martin had covered huge canvasses with biblical scenes of orgiastic frenzy, in which human depravity was displayed by crowds of semi-nude figures, carousing and cavorting in a landscape dark with impending doom. Particularly popular were Etty's *The World Before the Flood* and Martin's *Belshazzar's Feast*. Prints of paintings like these found their way into illustrated family bibles. They were also captured on coloured slides and displayed by 'magic lantern' in what became an early fore-runner of cinematic entertainment.

As in classical *Commedia Dell' Arte*, the genre of the Hollywood biblical epic developed its own stereotypes. One of these was the arch-villain, similar in many ways to pantomime's demon king. The type recurred as Nebuchadnezzar, Haman, Herod, Nero, Caligula or any one of a number of fictitious characters, created by Hollywood to supply what was wanting in the biblical text. It was necessary that the villain should be a grotesque – evil, insane and given to outbursts of terrible rage – but it was essential that he should never become entirely repulsive. Like Captain Hook he should retain a ghastly appeal.

Peter Ustinov's Nero in the 1951 remake of *Quo Vadis* was a scene-stealing monster who easily upstaged the Christians. In contrast with his beguiling wickedness, Robert Taylor and Deborah Kerr's piety appeared limp. Jay Robinson's Caligula in *The Robe,* and its sequel *Demetrius the Gladiator,* was exquisitely deranged. His camp posturing as he swirled his imperial cloak to settle himself upon the imperial seat in the senate, his strutting about the marble halls, his adenoidal whine and manic rage (quite understandable in the face of Richard Burton's irritatingly wooden Marcellus) set this apart as a truly great performance.

More understated, but no less appalling in its suave villainy, was George Sanders's playing of Saran of Gaza in *Samson and Delilah*. By this stage in his career Sanders had developed the type, familiar in Hollywood's casting, of the English cad – ex-public school (Harrow, or possibly Stowe), exquisitely mannered, beautifully tailored and rotten to the core. When Victor Mature's Samson brought the temple of Dagon crashing down upon the heads of the Philistine nobility, cinema audiences felt an additional *frisson* as George Sanders disappeared beneath a heap of falling masonry.

The other convention of the biblical epic was the presence in the plot of a beautiful woman and, if possible, a sub-plot of love requited or, better still, love denied. These were not always easy to find in the narrative of the Bible or in the recorded history of the early church. However, Hollywood's scriptwriters were able to meet the challenge. In DeMille's second version of *The Ten Commandments* (1956) Moses was loved by two beautiful women. One of them, an Egyptian princess, Nefertiri, tried her best to keep him in Egypt, so that he could develop a career in politics. 'You will be king of Egypt, and I will be your footstool,' she said. To which he replied, reasonably enough, 'The man stupid enough to use you as a footstool isn't wise enough to rule Egypt.' And *she* said, 'Oh Moses, Moses, you stubborn, splendid, adorable fool.'

What added piquancy to the presence of these women in the plot was that they were acted by famous Hollywood beauties. For the regular filmgoer in the 1940s and 1950s the glamour of the cinema's stars made it impossible to divorce the famous or notorious private life of the actress from the role she was playing. This, and an accurate knowledge of the other parts she had recently played on the screen, led to a certain amount of confusion in people's minds.

It was impossible, for example, for people who saw Hedy Lamarr as Delilah in *Samson and Delilah* (1949) to get out of their minds her recent role in *White Cargo* – a film set in the Congo, in which she had played the part of a mixed-race siren whose sultry beauty drove the white rubber planters mad with desire. Particularly memorable had been her line, uttered with heavy innuendo as she emerged semi-clad from the steaming jungle, 'I am… [*pause*] … Tondelayo.' Now the line was replaced by, 'The Philisteens be upon thee, Samson.'

Nor was it easy to forget, when watching Rita Hayworth performing her sensuous dance of the seven veils in the title role of *Salome* (1953), that here was the same woman who, not so long ago in *Gilda,* had performed a deft striptease (she had removed a glove) while delivering the show-stopping number 'Put the Blame on Mame, boys'.

Other moments of delight were provided by a procession of famous actors making unexpected and inappropriate appearances. John Wayne surprised us all, not least himself, when he appeared in *The Greatest Story ever Told,* improbably disguised as the centurion at the foot of the Cross. Edward G Robinson, invariably cast as a homburg-sporting, cigar-chomping Chicago hoodlum, seemed ill at ease in the land of Goshen. James Robertson Justice, in his pre-*Doctor in the House* days and so before he had perfected the role of the irascible Sir Lancelot Spratt, made an unconvincing appearance in *David and Bathsheba.* But the most inspired piece of miscasting never in fact reached the screen: DeMille's first choice for the part of Moses was William Boyd, famous for his role as Hopalong Cassidy.

The major challenge to any film director was how to cast God. His was, after all, the main role. Fortunately, the Judaeo-Christian tradition, then still basic to Hollywood culture, forbade any visual representation of the Almighty. In a medium like the cinema this was a great advantage. It meant that God could be shown indirectly, engaging in the film's action through the visible effects of his power, and we know from the Old Testament how spectacularly cinematic those effects could be. Divine intervention in the form of earthquake, flood, drought, pestilence and falling masonry was the customary role allocated to God in the script. It had the merit of being a dramatic as well as convincing proof of divine authority (but not everyone was impressed – there is a scene during God's destruction of Sodom and Gomorrah where, amidst falling ceilings and shrieking extras, Queen Bera apologises to her guests for the changeable weather: 'Just one of our summer storms,' she drawls. 'It will pass.').

It was the New Testament that posed the greater challenge. God's role was now human. The Gospel required an actor to play Christ. There was, until the 1960s, a reluctance to portray Christ on the screen (the 1927 silent version of *King of Kings* had been exceptional). Hollywood devised a way of meeting this difficulty by presenting epics of the Christian era, in which Christ is unseen, or almost unseen, while remaining the ultimate hero of the story. *Quo Vadis*, *The Sign of the Cross*, *The Robe*, and *Ben-Hur* were all intended to be stories about Our Lord, but, as in the Old Testament epics, the invisible presence was depicted through his visible effects. Significantly, the 1925 silent version of *Ben-Hur* was entitled *Ben-Hur: A Tale of The Christ*.

For many people this oblique way of depicting Christ was more real, and closer to a genuine religious experience, than any attempt to present on film the Gospel story itself. This has nothing to do with the fear of sacrilege. Nor is it because the first two major attempts to put Christ's life on the cinema screen (*King of Kings* in 1961 and *The Greatest Story ever Told* in 1965) were such heavy-going. It has to do with the nature of the subject itself.

An inevitable consequence of treating the Gospel as source material for a biopic is that it remains just that: a biopic. What we are left with is the story of a first-century Palestinian Jew who became a revolutionary teacher and miracle worker, and suffered martyrdom at the hands of the authorities. The addition of the Resurrection at the end of the story – however sensitively done – never really convinces. In the context of biography it appears to be just an additional event in the life of Jesus, in the same continuum and on the same plane of experience as all the other events that have preceded it. This is also true of Pasolini's beautiful film, *The Gospel According to St Matthew* (1964).

For a dramatic presentation of the life of Christ to work, there has to be a way of making the audience feel, as the disciples did in their encounters with Jesus in Galilee, the transforming power of a presence which cannot be explained in terms of his biography alone. If it were possible to do it, the chronological episodes of his earthly life would have to be presented, not so much as stages in a narrative leading to death and resurrection but as events perceived through the prism of Easter and Pentecost. To do this there must be a reversal of that rule of dramatic narrative which requires the audience to exercise its suspension of disbelief by not 'knowing' the end of the story before the plot has reached its conclusion.

The Gospel narratives were written to be read with hindsight, to be understood within the context of post-Resurrection faith. The end of the story preceded the beginning. So far no film director has found a way of translating this into cinematic terms. Inevitably the camera sees the action through the eyes of a bystander in Galilee, Jerusalem and at Calvary, rather than through the eyes of the post-Pentecost Eucharistic community. The focus is wrong.

In the end, it may not be possible to present the Gospel story in a medium in which the emphasis is upon historical realism. Perhaps the closest we can get to a Life of Christ on the screen is indirectly through his redeeming effect on the lives of others. If that is so, the 1925 version of *Ben-Hur* was indeed correctly subtitled: *A Tale of The Christ.*

JOHN BETJEMAN

1906–1984
Poet Laureate

(First published in the *Church Times* to mark the centenary
of the poet's birth on 18 August 2006.)

'Betjeman, I shall be obliged if you will remove those bicycle clips from your ears.' It was 1940 and there was a war on. Kenneth 'Civilisation' Clark, who had been seconded from his post of Director of the National Gallery to be head of the films division of the Ministry of Information, was addressing a staff meeting when he paused to rebuke the future poet laureate. He himself had chosen Betjeman to join his unit. 'I wanted his flexibility and originality of mind, and also his charm, because, essentially, ours was a public relations role.'

Originality of mind and charm came at a price. Not everyone was amused by Betjeman's japes. C S Lewis, his tutor at Oxford, wrote in exasperation, 'I have never heard you speak of any serious subject without a snigger.' Betjeman chose not to disclose the extent of his seriousness to this booming 'beer and baccy' don.

He learnt early to use satire, and sometimes buffoonery, as weapons. At Marlborough he and Anthony Blunt founded *The Heretick*, a subversive magazine whose purpose was to tease the 'establishment' and mock the hearties. Its motto, taken from the Book of Psalms, was 'Upon Philistia will I triumph'. They both carried their subversive activities into adult life, though operating in different spheres.

Betjeman conducted his first successful conservation campaign in the pages of the official school magazine, *The Marlburian*. A letter to the editors written by him under the pseudonym 'Alexander Pope' lamented the desecration of Lady Hertford's grotto, now used to store the college potatoes. The grotto had been praised by an obscure eighteenth-century poet, Stephen Duck, whom Betjeman enlisted in his campaign. It is unlikely that more than a handful of his contemporaries had noticed the grotto in the college grounds. None had heard of Duck.

Campaigns to save Rennie's Waterloo Bridge, Euston Arch, the Adam brothers' Adelphi, Southend pier, and St Pancras station were some of the many to benefit from his mixture of erudition lightly worn and waspish ridicule. Although not always successful, his energetic defence of hitherto unfashionable eighteenth- and nineteenth-century architecture opened our eyes and altered public taste.

The campaign to save Holy Trinity Church, Sloane Street, was one of his greatest successes. This building, by J D Sedding, and embellished by Edward Burne-Jones, William Morris and other leading figures of the Arts and Crafts movement, was threatened with demolition in the early 1970s. It was said by the church authorities to be too big, too expensive, too ugly and too empty. Betjeman's publicity campaign, assisted by drawings by Gavin Stamp, preserved it for future use. It is now the home of a thriving congregation.

Others before him had rediscovered the delights of Victorian design and craftsmanship, but it was his bubbling enthusiasm which made him such an effective advocate. People who may never have given such matters a second thought now began to look at the buildings around them – railway hotels, bridges, town halls, churches – and not only the buildings, but the detail: rainwater hoppers, railings, door handles.

Clark, himself the author of *The Gothic Revival* (1928), claimed that 'the most important name' in changing public opinion was Betjeman's, and that was not because he had written articles in learned journals, but because he *talked*. And how he talked!

It is a measure of his impact upon the British public that we all knew his voice and mannerisms – his carefully created informality, his rehearsed digressions, his occasional use of outdated slang ('my hat!') his affected pronunciation ('lorst'). He had an engaging trick of taking his television viewers by the arm and saying to them, 'Now, come over here; there's something I want you to look at.' It was a polished, rehearsed performance in which he made judicious use of scholarly research, anecdote and self-parody.

This extract from his commentary to a TV film he made in 1951 is typical. The film shows him wandering about the Wiltshire town of Devizes, then he stops and says, as if the idea had just occurred to him:

> *Oh, and I forgot this. The Bear 'otel in the marketplace, a relic of coaching days. Look at that ironwork. About 1800, I should think. And then follow along to the older part. Sir Thomas Lawrence, the portrait painter, was born here; his father was the innkeeper. I like that great fat lettering across the front.*

As early as 1932 he made his first radio broadcast. It was in a variety show in which, still quite unknown to the public, he was billed as 'Betjeman major, the highbrow of the Upper Fifth'. At this stage, unsure of his audience, he was unsure of his voice. He read two of his poems: *Westgate-on-Sea* and *The most popular girl in the school* ('It isn't the same at St Winifred's / Now Monica's left the school'). It was an uncertain beginning to his broadcasting career.

In 1946 an accounts official at the BBC commented in a memo, 'As Mr Betjeman is a speaker of great reputation and experience, I am wondering whether we could not consider putting his standard fee for a fifteen-minute talk up from ten guineas to twelve.'

He cultivated an eccentric diction and a wild laugh. Philip Larkin called it 'a back-of-the-pit horse-laugh, wide open, all teeth and creases'. Diction and laugh he used to good effect. At Marlborough they were his weapons of defence against the school bullies. His contemporary, the poet Louis MacNeice, recalled, 'Down the passage was a door with an inscription above it:

Here thou, Great Anna, whom three realms obey,
Dost sometimes counsel take, and sometimes tea.

And inside sat John Betjeman writing nonsense on his typewriter or polishing his leather books with boot polish... a triumphant misfit. I felt ill-at-ease with him, not understanding his passion for minor poetry and misbegotten ornament.'

He remained a 'triumphant misfit'. As assistant editor in the early 1930s of the *Architectural Review* – a vehicle for the Modernist Movement – he was expected to promote the 'architectural nudism' of Le Corbusier. Instead, in an office hung with William Morris wallpaper, he wrote articles on his favourite figures of the arts and crafts school and *art nouveau* – C F A Voysey, Charles Rennie Mackintosh and George Walton. Maxwell Fry, the modernist architect, complained, 'I knew he would draw a facetious veil over our earnestness... as far as I was concerned, he was a bloody nuisance.'

Whatever the job, he stamped upon it his own personality. Often he would involve his friends. As editor of the Shell County Guides, a project which he initiated and which lasted thirty years, he enlisted the services of, amongst others, W H

Auden, Robert Byron, Peter Quennell, John and Myfanwy Piper, Lord Berners, a 'dissolute Irish peer' ('Cracky' Clonmore) and probably the last surviving squarson in England, the Reverend Henry Thorold.

He was posted to Eire during the war as the British Press Attaché in Dublin. It was thought that he would improve Anglo-Irish relations at a time when the German ambassador to that neutral country was making too favourable an impression. John Lehmann wrote of Betjeman's work in Dublin, 'He fulfilled his duties with immense aplomb and zest, charming the most suspicious among the local intelligentsia... and proving that in such a job a dram of personality is worth a hogshead of bureaucracy.'

Some of his success in Dublin was achieved in the Palace Bar, where in a smoke-filled inner sanctum he would meet people like the poet Patrick Kavanagh, R M Smyllie, the editor of the *Irish Times*, and the one-legged wit and raconteur, Tynan 'Pussy' O'Mahony, the father of the comedian Dave Allen.

After the war he became known to a wider public through his journalism, broadcasts and appearances on television. When we read his poetry, which we did in increasing numbers from the 1950s onwards, we could hear him speaking the lines. It was impossible to see upon the printed page the words of 'Indoor games near Newbury' or 'Death in Leamington' without hearing their author's voice.

This gave us immediate access to the heart of his poetry. It is this immediacy, together with his strong sense of place and time, which makes his verse so effective. The smell of the pines, the crunch of wheels on the gravel drive, the scent of gorse on the common, take us back to pre-war Berkshire and Surrey as surely as if we too had known them, as if we too had been in love with Pam ('you great big mountainous sports girl... you zephyr and khaki shorts girl') and been at school with her old Malvernian brother... you know, the one who plays tennis for Woking.

We do not need to have been alive in 1936 to be moved by his elegy, *The Death of King George V* ('Spirits of well-shot woodcock, partridge, snipe / Flutter and bear him up the Norfolk sky'), or to know instinctively just what he meant by the last verse with its reference to the new king's arrival in his capital:

> *Old men who never cheated, never doubted,*
> *Communicated monthly, sit and stare*
> *At the new suburb stretched beyond the run-way*
> *Where a young man lands hatless from the air.*

Nor need we have betrayed a wife to know the guilt of infidelity expressed in *Pershore Station:*

> *The train at Pershore station was waiting that Sunday night*
> *Gas light on the platform, in my carriage electric light...*
>
> *When sudden the waiting stillness shook with the ancient spells*
> *Of an older world than all our worlds in the sound of Pershore*
> *bells...*
>
> *With Guilt, Remorse, Eternity the void within me fills*
> *And I thought of her left behind me in the Herefordshire hills.*

He located the eternal themes of love, desire, fear, and guilt in the ordinary: a Bath teashop, Margate 1940, Harrow on the Hill, a bus stop. At times, especially when called to write official verse as Poet Laureate, his verse could be banal, but at its best his deliberate use of bathos hit its target.

He was a religious poet, not because he wrote out of Christian conviction, but because he wrote out of uncertainty.

He admitted that his fondness for the Church of England, her 'dim' eccentric ways, her ornaments, liturgy and architecture, did not touch the deeper things of faith:

> 'Twas not, I think, a conscious search for God
> That brought me to these dim forgotten fanes.
> Largely it was a longing for the past,
> With a slight sense of something unfulfilled;
> And yet another feeling drew me there,
> A sense of guilt increasing with the years…
> Thus were my London Sundays incomplete
> If unaccompanied by Evening Prayer.

(Summoned by Bells 1960)

'When most of the poems in my latest collection were written [*A Few Late Chrysanthemums*], I was the self-pitying victim of remorse, guilt and terror of death,' he wrote in 1954. One of the poems in this collection – *Church of England Thoughts* – dwells wistfully upon the externals of faith. As he listens to the bells ringing from the tower of Magdalen College, Oxford, he thinks of the slow progress of Matins and the 'elevation of the plate', of High Mass and churches 'blue with incense mist', of chapels-of-ease by railway lines, and 'country churches old and pale', where rugged hands ring changes on the bells.

But the blow falls in the last verse, with its distant echo of Matthew Arnold's *Dover Beach*:

> Before the spell begin to fail,
> Before the bells have lost their power,
> Before the grassy kingdom fade
> And Oxford traffic roar invade,
> I thank the bells of Magdalen Tower.

It is possible to read in these lines no more than a passing regret that the modern world has interrupted a summer reverie. But there seems to sound in them a more sombre note – Matthew Arnold's 'melancholy, long, withdrawing roar' as the tide of faith runs out.

'And is it true?' he asks in his poem 'Christmas'. 'And is it true, this most tremendous tale of all… The Maker of the stars and sea become a child on earth for me?' The poem is in the same metre as Charles Wesley's 'And can it be?' The same use is made of the rhetorical question. But where Wesley's hymn ends in triumphant acclamation – 'Bold I approach the eternal throne / And claim the crown, through Christ my own' – Betjeman's poem leaves the question unanswered. At first sight the last verse appears positive enough:

> *No love that in a family dwells…*
> *Can with this single Truth compare*
> *That God was Man in Palestine*
> *And lives to-day in Bread and Wine.*

But this affirmation hangs upon the conditional clause almost hidden in the preceding verse: 'And is it true? For if it is…' If it is.

Betjeman's desire was to believe. It was this and his lingering lack of certainty that engaged so many of his contemporaries and expressed for them a convincing spirituality. However, he has another claim to be called a religious poet, and this is evident in the majority of his poems which are not explicitly religious at all. He opened our eyes to the wonder, sadness and sanctity of the commonplace.

When Pope wrote of Queen Anne at Hampton Court that she 'sometimes counsel took, and sometimes tea' – Pope would have said 'tay' – he meant to deflate. When Betjeman used the same trick in his verse, he meant to celebrate. C S Lewis was quite wrong: Betjeman was a deeply serious man, and devout. It was not the tutor's fault, however, that his pupil should have worked so hard to conceal this from him. But then, this was the man who at the age of thirty-four put bicycle clips on his ears during a staff meeting and claimed in *Who's Who* that his hobby was dirt-track racing.

STANDING ON THE SHORE

(From a sermon preached at Evensong in Holy Trinity Church,
Guildford, on the Third Sunday of Lent, 1999.)

*Lord, let me know mine end and the number of my days: O
spare me a little that I may recover my strength, before I go
hence and be no more seen.*

Psalm 39

The psalm, from which the words of this evening's anthem
are taken, is a poignantly beautiful poem about the brevity of
life and the transience of human achievement. It is one of a
vast anthology of poems and songs – both sacred and secular
– which lament the shortness of our existence, but which
contrive to do so with such grace that they dress our mortality
in a mantle of great beauty.

*For man walketh in a vain shadow, and disquieteth himself
in vain: he heapeth up riches, and cannot tell who shall gather
them*

On the whole, the human spirit scales loftier heights when
she is sad than when she is happy. Even the very words we
use give sorrow a greater dignity than joy. The ponderous
sound of words like 'melancholy' and 'mournful' strike a
deeper resonance in the mind than do the brittle syllables of
their opposites: 'glad', 'happy', 'merry' and 'bright'. It is no
accident that the vocabulary of the aching heart is richer than
the language of the cheerful spirit.

Why is the human psyche so inclined to melancholy? It crops up, this melancholy, in the oddest places. Some years ago at Blair Castle in Scotland there was held the World Bagpipes Championship. Pipers came from far and wide to give of their best. The championship was sponsored by Glenfiddich, the famous whisky distillers.

One of the contestants was asked if he was not distracted by all the hoop-la and the bright advertising lights. Was he not fazed by the fiery liquor so generously dispensed by the sponsors? He considered the matter for some minutes, and then replied that once he had started piping nothing could distract him; as he began the long-drawn-out lament of a Highland *pibroch* he could hear nothing but the music, and could see nothing but his life, stretching out far, far ahead of him into the distance, and death awaiting him at the end.

Now that's a perspective which you and I could well share. It is no morbid fancy of an unbalanced mind to raise our eyes to that distant day (that last and everlasting day) when we shall die. It is, after all, the only certain conclusion to our life, and is no less natural than our birth. It is the terminus to which we all travel. Without it our earthly lives would be indeed inconclusive, an endless and meaningless succession of days and weeks and months and years. Oh, the boredom of it all!

Mindful of our mortality, it is no wonder that the human spirit, when it is in reflective mood, tends to see the dark winter's night which lies outside the warmth and comfort of the fragile little house which is our earthly life. You may know the words of the seventh-century Northumbrian warrior, recorded by Bede. The warrior was speaking to King Edwin and said:

When we compare the present life of man on earth with that time of which we have no knowledge, it seems to me like the swift flight of a single sparrow through the banqueting hall where you are sitting at dinner on a winter's day with your

thanes and counsellors. In the midst there is a comforting fire
to warm the hall; outside the storms of winter are raging. The
sparrow flies swiftly in through one door of the hall, and out
through another. While he is inside he is safe from the winter
storms, but after a few moments of comfort he vanishes from
sight into the wintry wind from which he came. Even so,
man appears on earth for a little while; but of what went
before this life or what follows, we know nothing.

Those words were spoken by an unnamed thane and recalled
by bystanders. A generation later they were recorded by the
historian Bede. They ring out across the centuries.

But there is another picture equally compelling as that of the
sparrow's brief flight. When Isaac Newton was dying he spoke
these words about his lifetime's achievement, about what lay
behind him in the past and the vast unknown which lay ahead:

I have been only like a boy playing on the seashore and
diverting myself in now and then finding a smoother pebble
or prettier shell than ordinary, whilst the great ocean of truth
lay all undiscovered before me.

When we stand upon the shore, as every day of this uncertain
life we stand upon its edge, and as we busy ourselves with the
cares and pleasures and pains of this lovely world, picking over
the pebbles and the shells, there sounds in our ears the distant
roar of that great ocean of unknown truth which lies at the
rim of our brief lives. What else then can we do but pray in the
words of the psalmist:

Lord, let me know mine end and the number of my days: O
spare me a little that I may recover my strength, before I go
hence and be nor more seen.

ACKNOWLEDGEMENTS

Thanks are due to the editor of the *Church Times* for permission to reprint articles which originally appeared in that journal, to the editor of RSCM *World of Music 1986* for permission to reprint the article, *Athelstan Riley*, to Mr Graham Norton for permission to quote words from his column in the *Saturday Telegraph*, and to the Earl and Countess De La Warr for permission to publish an account of a visit to the Sackville family vault.

ALSO BY ADRIAN LEAK

Nebuchadnezzar's Marmalade Pot

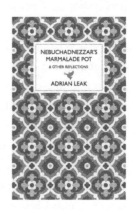

Brief, sharp, witty and profound – these reflections are in the best pastoral tradition of the Church of England – they make us chuckle, help us think and show us a glimpse of 'heaven in ordinary'.

Angela Tilby, Canon Emeritus of Christ Church, Oxford

It was George Herbert who noted that the good country parson is 'a diligent observer and tracker of God's ways', setting up 'as many encouragements to goodness' as possible. There could not be a better description of Adrian Leak who, in this wise and accessible collection of reflections, holds a compass that guides us through both the Church's year and the seasons of the heart. Celebrating the richness of the ordinary, he helps us appreciate that, at the end of the day, Christians are called to nurture the human capacity to look and to love.

Mark Oakley, Canon Chancellor of St Paul's Cathedral, London

Adrian Leak's brilliantly observed reflections make a fascinating read. They will appeal not only to Anglicans, including lapsed ones, but also to the large number of people who, while they have not been blessed with the gift of faith, care deeply for the Church of England. Adrian draws his inspiration initially from apparently superficial incidents and details, but as he gets drawn in he plumbs the depths and writes most movingly about the spiritual life and the problems of pursuing it in a largely indifferent and often hostile world. He claims his reflections are merely random meditations, but in fact they display the workings of a profound and mature intelligence.

Roger Lockyer, Reader Emeritus in History in the University of London

Archbishop Benson's Humming Top

Archbishop Benson's Hummingtop
propels us from Greek hats to gardens, via
compassion fatigue and hunting parsons to
the songbirds of Istanbul. Underpinning
and uniting these wide-ranging reflections
is the conviction that God is to be found
in stillness and silence, and that we need
to be able to listen if we are to hear the
still, small voice. Adrian Leak has created a box of delights: quirky
and thoughtful, with plenty of still centres, to be dipped into and
savoured: nourishment for the soul, with no damage to the waistline.

Caroline Chartres, *Features Editor, Church Times*

There is always grace, eloquence and wisdom in Adrian Leak's
writing. He offers reflections on simple, familiar matters with poetic
richness. Common sense, such as Adrian has in abundance, is as
rare as it is valuable. It has been said "As the tribe is dying, the dance
gets faster". Adrian shows a different way: how by paying respect to
others, we grow in confidence; how humanity is a step on the path
to resilience. These characteristics are needed (as much as they are
under-valued) in the church today. This is a book of gentle, honest
and grace-filled hope.

Robert Cotton, *Rector of Holy Trinity, Guildford*